Admar Rene De Sousa

THE CODE OF SEX & *Infidelity*

BlueRose Publishers

First Published in September 2020

ISBN: 978-93-5347-915-2

BLUEROSE PUBLISHERS

www.bluerosepublishers.com

info@bluerosepublishers.com

+91 8882 898 898

Cover Design:

Mohit Joshi

Typographic Design:

Teena Maurya

Distributed by: BlueRose, Amazon, Flipkart, Shopclues

About the Author

Despite the horrible fact that my mother left me for dead in a chicken den; I believe that man is a dynamic being living in a dynamic world full of undiscovered mysteries that hold vital and crucial keys to both mundane and divine spiritual success. I am 29 years of age and have come far in my walk with God that started in the year 2007 but officially launched in the year 2012 under one of the most powerful seasons on the calendar of God known as Revival. A man is dynamic hence, we are more than one thing and are more than capable to achieve greatness, even the impossible if we are focused or deeply rooted in Christ Jesus, who is the bridge to both the physical and spiritual world.

I believe that I am more than a preacher of the word of God and have much to share with the world; hence, man is a dynamic being living in a dynamic world. The greatest enemy, rather the greatest strength and weakness is your very own body if left unchecked, it will destroy you if your eyes are not opened. One of my dynamics understands the human body and that extends to women in general not just a matter of the dating life.

This book only entails my personal experiences with dating pertaining my youth to presently seeking a suitable partner to settle with. Thus, this is my journey other than the mission in serving Christ as God Himself states; ***"it is not good that man should be alone; I will make him a help meet for him."*** One of our dynamics as men is the fact that we need women in our lives otherwise, we lack something beyond our comprehension.

You Tube Creator: Redeemed Phoenix

Instagram: instagram.com/redeemed_phoenix/

Blog: poeticwolfblog.wordpress.com

Poetry Collection: Watt pad (Redeemed Phoenix)

Acknowledgement

First, I would like to thank my cousin ***Alexandrea De Sousa*** for all the support and motivation for helping me achieve my writing goal. At the same time, I am also thankful for my best friend ***Natasha Dassu*** who connected me to a very talented Graphics Designer, ***Rani Smith*** who I humbly thank for my Book cover page and paper back. Finally yet importantly, this book would not have reached the finish line without the guidance and direction of ***Dr. Hardik Joshi*** to publish under *Blue Rose.* Most importantly, not forgetting the woman who raised me**,** ***Graziela De Sousa.*** Through her, I made it to Higher Education from childhood hence, today if I stand as a Poet, Writer and a Blogger she is the force behind my linguistic success. The rest I owe to **God** as my talents belong to **Him** alone.

Table of Contents

Introduction

To establish **Why Women Cheat,** I have laid the foundation as follows. Cheating in all cases comes with no valid excuse. If it were not for my very first experience in the year **2017**, where I actually put my heart in it, I would still be of the player image taking pride on the women I hurt. I always knew **Karma** would catch up to me but not in that magnitude. I have no words to explain the pain I felt, but one thing remained outstanding; cheating is no fun. It is dangerous and costly, both to the present and future relationships.

Every person that falls victim to infidelity needs some form of counselling not to say that they are crazy but the heart has been broken and healing needs to take place. Aside from healing, trust has also been broken which affects future relationships as trust is the entire basic focus of a happy relationship.

Where there is no trust there is no peace, and where there is no peace; there is anxiety and worry, which in the end leads to a very stressful relationship birthing quarrels as nothing, but fights will be the peak of that relationship. In my case, I developed a principle whereby, I would always prioritize my heart, and cheating in the early stages of the relationship was my ultimate safeguard against any form of heartache and most especially being cheated on. I for one never wanted the female coming to me crying that she made a mistake by sleeping with another person. I never ever wanted that pain but funny enough I have had two relationships in which I never slept with the girls but they cheated on me with several people and this was right after my first love broke up with me because of her **"Jealous-Friends".**

Now you can imagine the pain I was carrying. Even as I dated those two serious cheaters, I still had strong feelings for my first love. Her name is "Eve" and I still remember her beautiful name. It took me five long good years to get over her. **Dating** for me became a living hell as I was always in misery; from Eve to the next two cheaters. I was never much into sex with these three in fact not at all, as I was a virgin. **Eve** and I were the best couple in comparison to every other female that I mingled with at that time. She is a strong believer and I at the time was just a mere Christian who had only recently received **Jesus** as Lord and Savior in the year **2007**. Now, the two cheaters really damaged my life and view on women but I learnt a lot from them about dating and women's wants.

If there are certain things, a woman wants in her man and when she cannot find that very thing - she will begin searching for it in another man subconsciously; it will happen as attention is first discovered in the back of the mind. As human beings, we tend to pay more attention to anything that triggers the interest of our minds. This **"Attention- Factor"** will be discussed in a separate chapter in detail. For the longest of years, I totally had no experience in the dating world and what hurt the most was the fact that I had older cousins and friends who were so good with girls. I remember being so curious, I mean one friend named Tally, God forgive me but he is terribly ugly and to my surprise, he had managed to date one of the most beautiful girls in Elma High School found in Blantyre City, Malawi.

I used to ponder on the question often but how? How does he do it and what does he say? These were my most innocent and deeply curious questions; that I picked up as an infant. I truly was that one cousin or friend that completely had no **A-Game** with women. The funny thing is that most women really liked me in all schools that I have been enrolled but this boy was never at the top of His **"A-Game,"** so I could never really pick up on the signs whether or not a girl was interested in me. Travel and socializing with these **"Alpha-Males"** began my conquest with woman. Another factor, which boosted my **"A-Game,"** lied in the fact that two cheaters broke my already wounded heart and that is the day I made up my mind to return the favor as my heart grew cold and distant from feelings necessary to keep a relationship flowing good in satisfactory romance. I became **"The-Beast,"** my mission was to conquer hearts, once they fell in love my next step was to gain their trust and in the end, break them all down to pieces that would never again rise the same. Truth be told what I became was something else.

To establish why men cheat? It is necessary that we look into Volume 1, ***Why Women Cheat? The Truth (Universal Cheating Signs).***

This Book? Is the product of the benevolent force that was awakened within the hearts of women from various countries as they personally asked me to write why men cheat? The Ladies were both inflamed and curiously interested to know exactly why men cheat.

In the end, this book will aim to direct all readers to nothing but the truth when it comes to infidel men and women, as well as the various main reasons as to why people cheat in the first place, and why men continue to cheat with no disregard to the love that they have or possessed to their dearly loved or unloved partners.

What needs to be said is that, this book is written with my heartfelt sorrow for all the mistreated women somewhere out there ***suffering in the hands of a cruel and heartless-bewildered- man***. It is without a doubt and perfectly clear that the majority of cheating cases lay in the hands of men. According to a survey done in the year 2017 by Patrick Wanis, America's number one celebrity life coach, the findings were as follows, *"man cheat at a higher rate than women, 22% versus 14%."*

In other words, there is a great gap between cheating men and cheating women being an estimated 8% dissimilarity a s not all women cheat but at the same time ***"not all men cheat,"*** and ***"not all men are men"***. There is so much truth in that saying. Somewhere out there exists men in their late thirties and forties who still struggle to place ***a decent meal on the table.***

Let us get real, life is hard and we need not judge one another but rather give a helping hand where best we can and that is ***the power within us that keeps us human.*** I really hope that you enjoyed why women cheat and that the knowledge you have attained has shed some insight in your life, I hope that where you were blind you now see and where you lacked you now have and where you viewed God as distant you now know He cares for you. It is all just a matter of acquiring hidden consciousness that will change your perspectives.

The sequential series of hard work bound together along with the sincere research on the subject *"cheating,"* all in the name off my readers. I wholeheartedly write in good faith and honestly seek to give you a great and understanding well-established read on the matter at hand.

Cheating is a growing trend and widely debatable as it has come undone or rather best put in the following words, relationship betrayals all have their reasons. The same way people back stab or gossip about one another is the same way we end up cheating on each other. With gossip "there is no smoke without fire," simply put there is a reason to everything that happens in life. There is a reason I was cheated on and there is a reason you were cheated on, and finally there is a reason you are still living in infidelity.

I will repeat those words once again, "everything happens for a reason." In every reaction there is a **cause-and-effect** thus, before the effect comes there was something that you as the partner either failed to do or provoked the chain reaction with fire that stimulated **the-mental-trap** that led to your severe heart ache. There is a reason why you were born in the family to which you were birthed and raised, there is a reason you went to all the schools you attended and if you never schooled in your life or recently dropped out due to any other reasons, money inclusive; don't worry. There is a reason! All will be well in due time.

If you are not getting that promotion you so desperately want at work, if you are struggling to be with that very beautiful girl that you've had your eye on for the longest, my brother, my sister don't worry, there is a reason to all our efforts that seem to come undone or cursed. However, there is no justification when it comes to cheating, be it the male or the female such a betrayal strikes deeper than the skin tearing through the heart and even surpassing the core of one's soul. Let me illustrate clarity. In all that, we do whether good or bad, intimacy should never be violated.

CHAPTER ONE

Rising Female Infidelity

According to psychologist **David J Ley Ph.D.** In his blog, titled (Women who stray) he has this to say; *"Lately, the media is filled with stories of cheating husbands. However, a bigger story is in the rising numbers of female infidelity. Every day, more women are having sex with men other than their husband. Younger women, under 25, and women over the age of 60 are cheating more than ever before."*

In this, 21st Century women have this application called WhatsApp Sex, which is dedicated solely to married women whom their husbands cannot satisfy which we will get into later on. To be honest all these dating apps come with infidelity to some extent and all are hell bent on secrecy and confidentiality being their number one policy to strictly follow. As we advance, we will look into the curses

of fornication and adultery, which include sleeping around with married persons. In some countries which I cannot dare to mention by name, the adoption of sleeping with married women has become a highly underground well-paying business whereby married couples allow the women to be sexually satisfied by strangers for lack of competence in bed which includes micro penises and lack of sexual education as well as foreplay and excitement.

To further back up his point, which I totally agree with, I believe we are living the biblical last days where it has been prophesied to be the darkest of ages. We now live in a generation where most people have no souls, we live in a world where entertainment is actually great evils and very stupid things, and people are no longer interested in helping themselves or others in achieving a better version of one self. We are strangely caught up with **The-Media-Life;** trying so desperately to become someone else entirely different from what we actually are deep inside our true nature. The **Media Life** is explained as follows; People are different and we all want different things from one another. Some just want sex, others just want money. In this day and age not many look for what's inside but rather focus on the external things given in life. It is sad to know that many are now dating for the wrong reasons. In truth, the reason most people get involved is because they look at what this person has and in what way will it benefit them. In most developing countries, women do not date men who do not have money, as they want the media life.

They want people with cars, bikes and houses, they are in it for the fame and fashion, these are the traits that blind us. Sadly; the universal reality of actually finding and falling in love with the right person has become a dream for most of our lives. The modern day trend places so much emphasis on first finishing school and then achieving the money to then settle with the women. If we are blinded by the physical world how then will God give Adam his Eve and vice-versa. Start training your eyes to see people for who they are and not for what they have.

The concept most women carry that "Money-Is-Love" whereby, if the male is not spending a dime on her even if she knows his financial situation is not good, "he doesn't love me" is the justification. Many gurus can agree with me that once you show a woman your wallet your relationship is doomed thus the saying, "a woman should never know your salary" on the other hand men carry the concept that, "Sex-Is-Love." This is an idea that will leave you miserable not too long from the start of your relationship. Women are not men, bare that in mind. They are simply not as sexually active as men and are certainly not as open about sex in comparison to men. Nevertheless, the thing is not all women are the same we very well know that people are different entirely.

In **David J Ley's** findings he also has this to say; *"Male infidelity, estimated between 50-60% of all males across a lifetime, has remained relatively steady. But female infidelity has progressively increased, to the point where current estimates put it between 45-55% for lifetime risk of infidelity by a woman, and some researchers suggest that female infidelity may one day rival male cheating. So why have we seen such a dramatic increase in such a relatively short period of time?* In my response to such a question, I would say, according to his findings in the first paragraph above, women were severely attacked and put in line by brutal force dating back to the beginning of creation which was unfair on them. Women were created to be a help unto men by God according to the book of Genesis thus, in actual sense, they are our equals and we need them to strive and be merry. I love women and cannot imagine a world without them, such a planet would be hell and tedious if I am to be utmost sincere.

David J Ley's response to his own question is as follows; "*First, I'm not sure that the rates of actual female infidelity are increasing as much as we think. What might be increasing is our awareness of it. For thousands of years, women have suffered horrific social punishments when caught in infidelity. Unfaithful women were raped, prostituted, beaten, mutilated, ostracized and killed by brutal means, from strangulation to stoning. Even in the past hundred years of increasing sexuality research and knowledge, infidelity has remained a very secretive behavior, especially for women. Estimates of infidelity are still widely regarded as suppressed estimates, due to the fear and shame people have about acknowledging past unfaithful sexual behavior.*"

In conclusion, David and I are on the same verdict concerning the rise of female infidelity. Women are more **Open-and-Free** due to the rise in feminist revolutions and writers in their struggles to achieve equal rights among a male dominated society that governs how and when exactly a woman may breathe or even move. The sphere we live in strictly rules out what is right and proper as well as what is improper conduct for a woman, since childhood woman have had to be beaten in check/line and follow a system that steers them into a mental crisis of depression and unspoken pain. The structure is messed up and nowadays a woman and a man struggle to trust each other as we have been brain washed to view women in a certain way thus, anything a lady may or may not do we tend to rush into judgement and often get angry. We evaluate a woman using a brain washed structure of thinking which in actual sense never allows the female to just breathe and be her natural self around men.

The problem with not accepting a woman for being different is catastrophic in nature. Just because a female likes to wear jeans she is abused, just because she likes to wear a mini skirt she is slandered, accused, beaten and even raped. Why are we violating our women for being who they want to be? Women are brainwashed to see a heartless man before they open up their hearts and males are brain washed to see nothing but a cheap whore when they look into the eyes of a woman. In the end, we both generally do not confide in the other as life has beaten us and shaped us unfairly. To further shed some light I have noticed that even among women they judge each other and call one another vile names. My granny is one example as funny as that sounds, it's sad really. No one was ever good enough and they were called all sorts of names be it English and other languages.

We need to be more open-minded and remember to love. Deep down beneath all that hard shell, yes even the males and females that pretend to be so tough, we all need love we crave to be wanted and accepted by others however, there is a normal and abnormal level of being accepted. What do I mean? Well, if any individual tries too hard or harder than normally prescribed to be received by any circle, be it open or closed groups then there is a problem. That generally means the individual trying too hard is not being true to himself and truth be told, no one wants be associated with a fake face.

Allow me to quote David's conclusion on the subject matter at hand. He states; *"In recent years, more people view infidelity as common, understandable, even normal and expected. In a survey by the* ***AARP****, only around 22% of respondents felt that infidelity was wrong, compared with a rate of 41% when this question was assessed* *in 1999. So, it may simply be that we are hearing more about infidelity, not because it's happening more, but because it is safer to talk about."*

In the same survey taken in New York - It was discovered that, *"Americans 45 and older are far more open to sex outside of marriage than they were 10 years ago, but they're engaging in sex less often and with less satisfaction, according to a major new survey by* ***AARP.****"* Bottom line is that mankind in this dark age is frustrated with the burdens of life, but the fact remains the same, the further one's soul drifts away from God and ventures in the exploration of sin and distractions, his purity will begin to fade right before his or her eyes dismantling unnoticed to the naked eye way before it's even too late to start getting back on track. Human beings were created to fellowship with the creator of both heaven and earth therefore; the only being that can truly take away the emptiness that you feel is Jehovah God through His only begotten Son, Jesus Christ the Savior of humanity.

Life becomes harder and only more frustrating as nothing will please you; not even fulfilling your life's purpose will have any meaning as you abandoned it a while back to pursue the media or some other form of futile pride. Vanity will be your very remnant, and at the road block of your existence you will face the final dead end, the same road you chose to walk away from God. You have forgotten that hell exists and the paragraph has come to your attention like a hot slap to your face. Wake up! Keep reading, ***"do not be afraid,"*** there is hope for you.

In conclusion to this chapter, women, better think twice before calling men *"dogs."* After all according to the survey's mentioned above as well as the accuracy in historical events we can clearly note that half of the men that cheat do not act by themselves but with women who know very well what they are doing (Sleeping with taken men). The data clearly shows us that women are just as bad in comparison to men. However, more than this, women might actually soon overtake men in the cheating game. This information and research was gathered in 2009.

CHAPTER TWO

Are Women More Forgiving than Men?

According to results from London, by Jargan Post Editorial; It was discovered to hold the same ideals and beliefs as well as understanding that I hold as, "most women are likely to forgive their partners for cheating once or twice, but only one in ten men would stay with a woman who had strayed." A new UK survey has found that, "more than six in ten women would forgive two relationship 'errors' which include infidelity, excessive flirtatious behavior or romantic neglect. They would, however, dump their man after three."

The Daily Mail reported the poll of 2,000 British men and women by laundry specialists Dr. Beckmann found that, "a full 53% of women said they would give their partners another chance even if they found out they had cheated on them, as long as that cheating was a one-time thing and didn't involve a pro-longed affair."

On the other hand, *"only 13% of men would stay with their partner if they discovered they had been cheated on. Some 89% of the 2,000 men and women surveyed said unfaithfulness was the most difficult problem to recover from in a relationship."*

Lack of intimacy and romance and partners spending too much time with their friends or at work are among the top bugbears from men and women in relationships. 38% of all current British relationships have endured infidelity of some kind, according to the study.

I would like to point out the major difference among the two when it comes to forgiveness coming from the male in regards to the women cheating. There is no truth in a "Cheating-Women." Unlike "Cheating-Men," when we cheat we feel bad and simply apologize looking for genuine forgiveness. Whether we are caught or not; a real man looks for forgiveness, that is all. It is as plain and simple as it gets. Yes, we do fear losing the love of our lives but there is no point holding on to a lie in a relationship. A lie will always catch up to you and by the time it does, it grows becoming worse than before thereby, producing a greater outcome that could have easily been forgotten. I mean the time it takes to start investigating whether she cheated or not only starts to strain on the trust; the more time passes the more the trust is lost and what's a relationship without trust? Women in the end fail to come clean when they are in the wrong, which is unfair despite how they feel, the truth sets us free.

The major reason cited for the relationship's subsequent survival is that, following the infidelity, both partners have agreed to be *"honest, frank and open about their feelings".* **Maintaining-a-Relationship** and the **Seven-Key- Elements** teaches us how best flow in accord with one another. In the most straightforward manner of explanation, a relationship is a Decision to be with someone you like. That liking grows and turns to love. What gives the strengthening foundation to a relationship is "trust." What a healthy relationship needs is; "communication, openness, dates, space, respect, responsibility and finally, some good sex." of course not before marriage, but hey! This generation is too wild and everyone is too busy minding his or her own business. Not that I'm judging anyone. As I said earlier on, communication is key when dating. I mean only humans have been blessed with the gift of speaking as animals do communicate as well. Transparency I for one adore as the bible says; "do unto others as you'd like the same done unto you."

I do not want a girl that never tells me why she is late or where she is going, not that I do not trust her but it is sacredly essential to maintaining a healthy relationship. Imagine your partner goes out to let us say a party. She arrives and never says a word just to show up home the next day. This takes us to the next point, respect. Both partners need to pay attention to each other and be really good listeners as this will help avoid future fights and arguments.

Imagine telling the most important story of your life to someone who either will forget or is simply not interested in what you have to say. Sometimes space is necessary to help you miss each other despite the strong bond of craving each other every minute of every day. Maintain that desire that makes you excited for each other otherwise the beauty and the romance begins to fade right before your very eyes.

Going on dates is one of the most romantic ways to add dynamic fuel to your love life.

A separate day that becomes a pattern for a date night will brighten both your days with a pure joy that comes from the universe itself. Responsibility is critical just as much if not even more than the rest. Truth be told both parties have a role to play and no one wants to be with an immature adult. I will say it again with a smile, some good sex is just as healthy as it gets. Others know it as lovemaking. The question now is what is sex? Sex is the union of body and soul, an intimate fusion of two separate beings becoming one body. It is a powerful universal connection whereby all that makes up your partner; the good and the bad, you are saying, baby, it is okay! I accept you for who you are entirely. Give me all of you as I give you all of me. Take my entire burden and all my anxiety; I live with and for you from now on.

I am happy I am home. A relation with no sex is frustrating to the soul as one can feel loneliness and abandonment, as sex is acceptance. A relationship without all the above will have its ups and downs, but even if one or the other fails, remember not to give up or call each other names as both of you are adult enough and chose by your own free will to venture into love. If I'm to be frank I had a major problem with women when it came to my personal perception of my woman and what I desire her to be like, the same way all real women have a **list** which will be discussed in great detail towards the ending chapters. I too have my very own personal list and after close observation I noticed the undeniable, the moment my subconscious mind *rang the alert button* my conscious mind reacts constantly by telling me she won't survive if I show her an extra 30% of my persona and it is at that moment my mind is made up to end the relationship despite the woman not having even the slightest symptoms of cheating. I just get disturbed and honestly run away from the responsibility of having to continue living a lie and deceiving myself that I am happy with the person. To be further sincere I discovered after pondering on the situations concerning why certain events become what they become I came up with my very own **Theory-of-Sex** which involves **10/30** principle in which a great void is created within the early stages of almost every relationship that ends in serious negativity.

This is my Theory of sex:

In connection to the *Attention-Factor* discussed in **Chapter Four; first Volume of Universal Cheating Signs, Why Women Cheat?** I believe the very first time we see any person of interest (the opposite sex) we pick an interest in which we only give off or show **10%** of what we feel, as our emotions are to be unlocked. Let us agree to disagree with those who live in a fantasy that there is, *"no such thing as love at first site"* which may only exist in a fairy tale. The feeling of love at first site is nothing other than our primal instinct's operating under the **influence of lust** which boils at two variable degrees being cosmic and intangible or supernal in nature.

It is from this point that both species feel this degree of 10% emotion radiating in the room and for some reason the second sign is eye contact, which can get very weird in a very short time if the male does not respond in the heat of the moment as an **Alpha.** At this point, the female will either make it obvious or pretend that she is looking by accident. Other signs that follow up are a heightened level of speech and whether or not she is playing with her hair and those beautiful smiles. Failure to seal the deal here means the male is registered as a **beta,** meaning the green light has turned red. Approaching her minutes, hours or even days later will be like seeking for directions to the bathroom.

Now for the Alpha that knows what he is doing this is the **initiation stage** where nothing but conversation must take place with very minimum pickup lines, women are not stupid! Success from here means quality time at the movies I mean yay you just got your first date, high five and celebration time. Men value women whether we are jerks or not we love women hence, we spoil them in whatever way we can even if that means we know we stand no chance but we will always go the extra mile and sob in the end when we fail and have our **egos broken.** Now at this stage I believe we open up **30%** towards the female of interest, and vice versa if the women is not just there to suck your money for the fun of her boredom.

Now pay attention as I expand on my working proven theory countless times of study and observation. All relationships fail because one person, whether the man or the women gives up because of the list of requirements. This has always been my mistake and the mistake of many men. After the first date depending on the man, being an Alpha or a Beta the possibility of intimacy may or may not be given. Now for the Alpha we already know the heat of the moment is obvious.

After the completion of the 10/30 Principle law of Attraction, **A Great Void** is created in which the emotions are fully open for the female and not the male but still a great void remains. It is here that most males fall under the power of a women, remember sex is power and the penis goes into the vagina in other words the man is sucked in and when he release his energy through an orgasm he surrenders power/ energy. According to **Psychologist Katarina Gabrova,** *"sex* *is about power."* Most man give even 110% leaving a gap of anything around **(30-100).**

To elaborate the principle I would like to say that even though men may say that a women is easy, let me point out that no women is easy to jump into bed with. If a women is found in such a position it means she has already made up her mind to be with that man. You see women are fast thinkers before they do anything they have already analyzed and scrutinized the entire situation. Which means you are lucky to fall into her list, which we will look into later.

Now the question is; what is sex and what does this great void do? This great void robs infinite hours of emotions, time, feelings and understanding. You become-bound as one i.e. a **Soul-Tie,** which will be looked into in the following chapter. In conclusion rushing into a relationship causes a great void which is dark and cruel, a breeding ground for all things negative and before you know it, sweet tender short term memories become bitter-cold, bipolar, long term mental traumatic nightmares to the point of regrets and frustrations that cannot be explained from a physical perception.

If a women is into you she will open up to you, this opening up is a form of accepting all that you are with all your baggage, known and unknown hence the question what is sex? As discussed and addressed under the subject Maintaining a relationship I revealed about 40-60% knowledge on the question and will certainly go the extra mile to shed more light on sex as we advance towards the end of the book. If you remember when I dealt with the

Concept, sex is love to men and money is love to women under the Media life, well now you know why sex is the solution for stress to most males. If a woman loves you then the gates to paradise are open. The number one sign a relationship is failing for men is when the gates are closed whether temporarily or permanently, it's a very serious concept which I would like to shed more light on the Three Pillars of a happy and healthy relationship that is not subject to the signs of cheating; mental, emotional health & spiritual balance.

CHAPTER THREE

Soul-Ties, Fornication & Adultery

A soul tie according to an Article by *MinisteringDeliverance.com* is; "*like a linkage in the soul realm between two people. It*

links their souls together, which can bring fourth either beneficial results or negative results."

The positive effect of a soul tie: The Article goes on to explain as follows; "in a godly marriage, God links the two together and the Bible tells us that they become one flesh. As a result, of them becoming one flesh, it binds them together and they will cleave onto one another in a unique way. The purpose of this cleaving is to build a very healthy, strong and close relationship between a man and a woman."

Matthew 19:5, *"And said, for this cause shall a man leave father and mother, and shall cleave to his wife: and they twain shall be one flesh."*

Soul ties can also be-found in close strong or close friendships. They are not just limited to marriage, as we can see with King David and Jonathan:

1 Samuel 18:1, *"And it came to pass, when he had made an end of speaking unto Saul, that the soul of Jonathan was knit with the soul of David, and Jonathan loved him as his own soul."*

In this context, the soul tie is a non- sexual one but rather a great bond of friendship. With this bond however even as good as, it may be once a betrayal unfolds, serious and unholy events may arise between two.

Best-friends as the thought remains the same, how could he/she betray me like this, after all I have done. In short, even the best of friends can go to war with one another because of a soul tie.

The negative effect of a soul tie: According to Kris who published, his Article on the date of February 3, 2016 had this to say on the subject; "Soul ties can also be used for the devil's advantage. Soul ties formed from sex outside of marriage causes a person to become defiled."

A relationship that constantly aborts is a sign of a bad/ unhealthy relationship in which the Devil has found a way in. Constant arguments over the most silly and petty things. Unexplained anger whereby there is never peace in the home. Couples that fight often even to the point of moving from verbal to physical action that leave the women crying bitterly. I will expand on this point later on.

Genesis 34:2-3, *"And when Shechem the son of Hamor the Hivite, prince of the country, saw her, he took her, and lay with her, and defiled her. And his soul cleaved unto Dinah the daughter of Jacob, and he loved the damsel, and spoke kindly unto the damsel."*

Through this act of evil, a whole Nation was later brought to death, utter eradication from the face of the world. As stated in why Women Cheat? A woman should never be forced into sex and any man that rapes a women should be put to death by law, but sometimes the law may be unfair as in a few cases the person may not be in his right mind, yes I'm talking about actual possession at this point. However as there is no room for God in the court of law how then can the judgement separate "Men's Rea" from actual Possession?

Kris further goes on to shed much more light when he says; *"In the end soul ties are the reason why it is so common for a person to still have 'feelings' towards an ex-lover that they have no right to be attracted to in that way. Even twenty years down the road, a person may still think of their first lover... even if he or she is across the country and has their own family, all because of a soul tie!"*

Demonic spirits can also take advantage of ungodly soul ties, and use them to transfer spirits between one people to another. The following Bible verse explains this concept clearly. ***Ezekiel 23:17,*** *"And the Babylonians came to her into the bed of love, and they defiled her with their whoredom, and she was polluted with them."*

Sex is a **tridimensional experience**: spirit, soul, and body. Anytime you have sex with a person you bond with them. **Dr. Daniel Amen** writes in his book, *"Change Your Brain, Change Your Life."* In the end, I highly agree with Kris,

"Whenever a person is sexually involved with another person, neurochemical changes occur in both their brains that encourage limbic, emotional bonding. Limbic bonding is the reason casual sex doesn't really work for most people on a whole mind and body level. Two people may decide to have sex 'just for the fun of it,' yet something is occurring on another level that they might not have decided on at all: sex **is enhancing an emotional bond between them whether they want it or not.** One person often the woman, is bound to form an attachment and will be hurt when a casual affair ends. One reason it is usually the woman who is hurt most is that the female limbic system is larger than the male's."

This is what we call soul ties. Sex is like gluing two pieces of wood together and the next day ripping them apart. Of course, wood from the opposite board remains on each board. A piece of your sex partner (the good, bad, and ugly) stays with you (and vice versa) for the rest of your life. You can only imagine what it looks like when you bond with multiple partners.

Unhealthy soul ties are often the ramifications of having partners that you create a life-long bond with through a sexual encounter(s), but with whom you only have a short-term relationship. The bond (soul tie) remains long after the relationship is over, leaving both sexual partners longing for wholeness.

THREE REASONS UNHEALTHY SOUL TIES TAKE

PLACE: According to kris;

1. People are misinformed and therefore convinced that sex is strictly a single-dimensional, physical act with no emotional or spiritual connections. **Yet after sex they**

find themselves mysteriously longing for the person, they may not even like.

2. A person (usually the woman) gives him or herself sexually to someone expecting that the intensely intimate act of intercourse would create a bond that would lead to deeper levels of commitment in their relationship. Once she discovers that her sexual partner was taking advantage of her need for intimacy and used her vulnerability of course; **this leads to a person being emotionally and spiritually bonded to somebody that they deeply resent!**

3. Two people commit to marriage and therefore surmise that the covenant vows are only a formality so they live together and enjoy a sexual relationship outside of a life-long commitment. Nevertheless, later they decide (for whatever reason) that they do not want to live in a covenant relationship and eventually break up. **They usually do not realize how deeply they have wounded each other as their souls are ripped apart, tearing the very fabric of their being in their separation.**

7 SIGNS THAT YOU HAVE AN UNHEALTHY SOUL TIE: according to kris;

1. "You are in a physically, and/or emotionally, and/or spiritually abusive relationship, but you "feel" so attached to them that you refuse to cut off the connection and set boundaries with them.

2. You have left a relationship (maybe long ago), but you think about the other person obsessively (you cannot get them out of your mind).

3. Whenever you do anything - make a decision, have a conversation with someone etc., you "feel" like this person is with you or watching you.

4. When you have sex with someone else (hopefully your husband or wife), you can hardly keep yourself from visualizing the person you have a soul tie with.
5. You take on the negative traits of the person that your soul is tied to and carry their offenses whether or not you actually agree with them.
6. You defend your right to stay in a relationship with the person that your soul is tied to, even though it is negatively affecting or even destroying the important relationships in your life (husband, wife, kids, leaders, etc.)
7. You have simultaneous experiences and/or "moods" as the person your soul is tied to. This can even include sickness, accidents, addictions etc.

1 Corinthians 6:15 - Do you not know that the one who joins himself to a prostitute is one body with her? For He says, "THE TWO SHALL BECOME ONE FLESH."

The problem with bonding souls to prostitutes is this, Prostitutes worldwide sleep around with men for money thus, the spirit of poverty, bondage and or indecency adapts to the person that sleeps with a prostitute, in other words when you make yourself one with a prostitute you become a prostitute and then you wonder why people want nothing to do with you. As the Bible is clear sex/intimacy, fornication or Adultery however you would like to put it brings about the same unchanging result which is the bonding of flesh into one flesh i.e. one person or one body thus, all problems experienced by one individual are either shared or become/ transferred to the other person making all problems one. I understand and know that this subject matter on Soul Ties has much more information to look into however; I only mention what is needed to shed an understanding in regards to the knowledge shared in this book. Coming this far I am certain you are experiencing many thoughts and evaluating your decisions in life and seeing the many mistakes and regrets of poor life choices and choices made out of innocence as well as old memories unlocking.

God is good and He is the ultimate healer. We all have a special season recorded in the Book of Life and unfortunate events and judgement recorded in the book of Death.

Hebrews 1:14

"Are not all angels ministering spirits sent to serve those who will inherit salvation?"

Salvation- does not just believe in Jesus Christ but a spiritual journey here on earth. To believe in Jesus is actually easy, I mean even the Muslims believe in Jesus, now why would I say this, sounds very mean and unbiblical and someone may argue the Muslims don't believe but yes they do believe in Jesus and His teachings but they are misled therefore are not saved. Now a Christian can believe in Jesus and still end up in Hell. I bet you want proof so look at this verse very carefully.

Mark 16:16 "*He that believeth and is baptized shall be saved; but he that believeth not shall be damned.*"

There are five baptisms but God is looking for three, Water (Submersion), Fire (Holy Spirit), & Persecution. Christianity is a journey that starts with believing in Jesus, his death and resurrection. **Romans Chapter 10 verses 8-13** Are the verses that changed my life and perception on Christianity from Atheism and Violence. There was a time I dreamed of becoming an Assassin to the point I was so caught up in it I began to love it and train under spirits how to kill by understanding the weak points of the human body.

I remember this one time in high school, we all have been there where the teacher asks everyone one by one to stand

and announce their dreams via a famous statement, "what would you like to be when you grow up?" my turn came and I declared out loud my dream of becoming a professional assassin with so much zeal and passion to only be criticized. Moreover, devastated. His name is **Mr. Mbale** Geography teacher. He said my dream is "stupid and he will not even laugh at such nonsense," I remember the entire class was laughing at me and I never even knew why at the time. The pain was humiliating thinking to myself why teacher would say that about my dream, I do not understand. Life is all about perception, until we share who we are with the world we might never really come to a point of self-awareness. His words and actions as well as many other people, family friends all helped direct my path to where I am today.

(Rev 20:12) "And I saw the dead, small and great, stand before God; and the books were opened: and another book was opened, which is the book of life: and the dead were judged out of those things, which were written in the books, according to their works." **(2Cor 5:10)** "For we must all appear before the judgment s eat of Christ; that every one may receive the things done in his body, according to that he hath done, whether it be good or bad."

To conclude on this chapter I am judging no one but giving knowledge to the World, how this wisdom is used is up to the freedom of choice (free will) we all have the power to decide the fate of our lives. I can only imagine when my time comes and my Angel presents my book, I mean I lost count how many women I slept with, let alone how many hearts I broke. God is merciful to those who love Him so I know my standing in His tender mercy and forgiveness. I am a Son of God and with no fear, I share the secret of knowledge and love through the book I present the code of sex and the laws that govern them. He that is wise will know exactly what to do with this gift.

I know that both these books will have a problem with many denominations but how long will we the Church keep our people in the **shadow of knowledge** by telling the children sex is wrong, sex is a sin, sex is immoral but deny them the knowledge of why it is wrong and how it affects them positively or negatively let alone deny them the teachings of Courtship before marriage forgetting the fact that before our children come to settle they first need to know their partners. Telling someone "do not" only pushes them towards the action to find out for themselves especially if appropriate reasons are not given.

New International Version 2 Timothy 3:1-5 1

"But mark this: There will be terrible times in the last days. 2
People will be lovers of themselves, lovers of money, boastful, proud, abusive, disobedient to their parents, ungrateful, unholy, 3 without love, unforgiving, slanderous, without self-control, brutal, not lovers of the good, 4 treacherous, rash, conceited, lovers of pleasure rather than lovers of God, 5 having a form of godliness but denying its power. Have nothing to do with such people." We are warned of the condition of our children so rather than force them, show them with love and wisdom why fornication is wrong and how it leads to sin and the results it births, which is the reason for this book. It is only fair, as children of this generation grow up faster and smarter.

CHAPTER FOUR

Salvation- how to successfully break a soul-tie:

The first thing we need to acknowledge is that we need God in this equation who sent down His only begotten Son Jesus Christ to die for our sins and through Him we have salvation and help in all things. God says He hates divorce and that is what a soul tie is once broken a separation of two people who lived in union as one body. Look at this with open mind, Romans 10:9-10 New International Version (NIV) 9 "if you declare with your mouth, "Jesus is Lord," and believe in your heart that God raised him from the dead, you will be saved. 10 For it is with your heart that you believe and are justified, and it is with your mouth that you profess your faith and are saved." There are two criteria's here, to be saved which means born again into the Kingdom of God.

The first is that you **confess with your mouth that Jesus is Lord*** which means Lord of my life and Lord of all, He is the King of kings. Second, you *believe in your heart that God raised Him from **The dead*** which means, you acknowledge the **power of God** and the fact that **"Jesus is Alive"** and presently living in Heaven at the right hand of God. Having understood this, it only means one thing; you are tired of feeling helpless and down and you have had enough of the voices in your head that tell you how unworthy of a person you are, You are not a failure and today is the day you understand How much God loves after all He sent His Son to die for you.

Anyone who is Born Again, a believer in Jesus Christ must know this verse if not then he or she are not born again but are living under the delusion of religion. Christianity is not a religion nor is it a denomination, there is one true God and His name is **Jehovah.** The error with the *Altar Call;* when the Pastor or Prophet stand representing Jesus and call sinners to the altar to give their lives to Jesus in order to receive new life many people make a mistake and as a result according to renowned Pastor Kenneth e Hagins who is no longer with us in this present age, Jesus Christ Himself appeared to him in a vision and elaborated the error with the Altar Call. Our Lord Jesus explained that people were dying and still going to **HELL** after the Altar Call.

After I carefully examined his vision and the words of Christ, I learned exactly what Jesus meant. The two criteria's to be saved involve Confession by mouth and believing with all your heart. Look at it this way, some can speak (confess) the words and not believe in the heart or someone can believe and not speak the right words. Someone can openly say Jesus is Lord and in his heart, there is no faith in what he is saying hence God is not mocked. To clarify any doubt allow me to explain it this way, many can agree with me that thousands do not really understand the power of salvation. What do I mean? Look at this, parents who force their children to go to church have also in like manner forced their children to walk down the Alter in response to the call to follow Jesus Christ and this is the result. Some in anger, some in fear, some in simply obedience obeyed their parents out of no choice and when the time comes to receive Jesus, the Pastor like a lost man with no discernment, no Holy Spirit, leads the sheep into condemnation and not salvation because they followed the instruction of what to say with their mouths (confession) but their hearts were far away from the truth and faith (believing) not even understanding the power of resurrection in which God Raised up Jesus from the grave.

Now that salvation is clear, the question is how do I receive Jesus or respond to the Altar Call the right way? Simply put you pray the sinners prayer to receive Jesus into your heart and life but before you do, first things first Jesus is pure and perfect He cannot **dwell** (live) in a **vessel** (body) that is unclean or full of sin that is **unconfessed sin**. Take time preferably **10 minutes** asking the **Holy Spirit to lead you** as pray and ask God to forgive of all your sins being known and unknown, confessed or unconfessed. One sign that the Holy Spirit is with you and guiding you is that some sins that your mind had blocked out even dating back to the Ages of five will be unlocked and as you remember them please mention them and surrender them to God.

I can only presume and believe in you that you followed the prophetic instruction and now you are finally ready to make the most important decision in your life, which is accepting Jesus as your Lord and Savior of your life. Follow this prayer and by the end of the last word being **Amen,** you will be saved, a born again Christian. Declare these words with faith and Power in Jesus Mighty Name!

The Salvation Prayer:

Lord Jesus Christ, I come before you with my life and all that I am, I Acknowledge that I am a sinner in need of eternal life, please cleanse me with your precious blood from all sin, every sin I have just mentioned and surrendered to you in Jesus Name. I confess that you are the messiah, I believe that you are the way the truth and the life and no one comes to the Father except through you. I believe with all my heart that God (Jehovah) raised you from the dead, I believe in the resurrection power, I give my life to you today, use me as you please, Lord Jesus I ask that you come into my life fill my heart and fill me with the Holy Spirit. Amen.

Now that you are born again and saved which means you have repented **(A complete turnaround)** you are now a new creature in Christ Jesus with a new Identity. I challenge you that all sorts of women will come after you even those women who you chased after for so long to no avail. Trust me stay away from them, they dangerous spirits who want to suck you dry. If you are a women flee (run) from those men that chase you nonstop even those ones that you crushed for so long and not once did they give you any attention, they are dangerous spirits after your new life in Jesus Christ. It will not be long from now, please be on guard not to fall.

I advise the need to find a church that will mentor you into maturity in Christ Jesus; the wolves in sheep's clothing are many and very hungry for your destruction. You have just entered a completely new realm a supernatural one to be precise. I am available on **You Tube:** Redeemed Phoenix.

Breaking Soul Ties Now:

According to Sheila Wray; "when we have a sexual experience, our brains produce dopamine, the same chemical that feeds a gambling addiction, your chocolate cravings and the junkie's need for another fix. Dopamine is often described as the "feel good" chemical of the brain and it plays a major role in our lives (good and bad)." Remember a soul tie is gluing two pieces of wood together and then ripping them apart. Meaning pieces from both sides will be mixed on all sides and that continues the more we create soul ties through fornication with several other persons which in the end leaves us lost, confused and in many cases severely depressed, yes there exists countless reasons for depression and soul ties are one of them. I remember how unhappy I was when Eve called off our relationship over a phone call while I was in Boarding School, to be honest I was hurt to the point I cried a couple of times it took me five solid years to naturally heal and get over her. I had no idea about soul ties back then and the most powerful thing about our love for each other, we never got intimate not once just real love. Now imagine if we actual made love by intimacy and formed an actual soul tie. What took me five years would have probably been a lifetime sentence of misery and pain I am certain one would have commit suicide. This is your chance now to break free from soul ties and fornication with the following guide.

Step #1 Acknowledge

First, we need to **acknowledge that there is a problem.** Ask the Lord to show you who you have ungodly soul ties with. Make a list if you need to. When I made mine, I was very shocked. Some of the men/women we fornicate with we do not even remember because that is how Satan operates in the Darkness. He does his things plotting your downfall in secret. Some soul ties are so ungodly they bind your life to failure just as some relationships are toxic and non- productive, they go nowhere just bound in misery.

Step #2 Repent of any sins that involve that person

Secondly, we need to **confess and repent of our sins**. This may involve finding a godly accountability partner that you can confess to and who can help you walk through the process. It maybe be a church counselor, pastor or elder or a family member. If you have had adultery, fornication, etc., it is vital that you repent of those sins and receive God's forgiveness for it before you can go about breaking the soul tie. Once you make your list, it is important to actually call some of the people you remember, maybe you hurt them so bad or vice versa healing and forgiveness must be released. Some people really hold you in their hearts, one of the reasons people do not succeed falls back to fornication and soul ties.

Step #3 Forgive the person of any wrongs done

Next, we need to find forgiveness. **We need to accept God's forgiveness, we need to forgive ourselves and lastly, we need to forgive our former partners or abusers**. According to **Sheila Wray**, "Un-forgiveness is like drinking poison and hoping the other person dies." If you have any un-forgiveness in your heart against the person, you must choose to release that bitterness and forgive the person. The Bible is clear that bitterness defiles a man. Some people carry a strong spirit of bitterness if they dare or have cursed you in pain you have been locked by that soul tie until they release you.

Step #4 Renounce any covenants made with the person

If you have made any spoken commitments, vows or even simply saying, "I will love you forever", it has ample power in the spiritual realm to bind the soul to that person (form a soul tie). The tongue is quite capable of binding the soul and can be a great means to create soul ties: I remember after discovering that marriage by certificate was nonsense I used the Christ given authority to officially be wed us and after months of separation while in prayer the Spirit of the Lord spoke to me reminding me to break those vows. I called her and we spoke breaking the soul tie and vows we made to one another. God takes fornication very serious. Will be looking into what constitutes a real marriage shortly.

***Proverbs 6:2**, "Thou art snared with the words of thy mouth, thou art taken with the words of thy mouth."*

These spoken covenants need to be renounced in order to break the soul tie. When you renounce something, you basically take them back verbally. You spoke them verbally, now it is time to take them back verbally. For example, if a woman has had a soul tie with a man who was not the one, and said she would never be able to love another man, then this needs to be renounced if she wants to break the soul tie. Such a woman could renounce it by saying something like, "I renounce having said that I will never be able to love another man."

Step #5 Burn/Throw away any gifts exchanged

You must also do an inventory and **remove any mementoes, gifts or souvenirs from those past relationships**. Gifts also symbolize a relationship and can hold a soul tie in

Place. If a person has a ring, personal gifts, cards, jewelry and other 'relationship gifts' from a previous relationship, then it is time to get rid of them. Holding onto such gifts symbolizes that the relationship is still in good standing and can actually hold the soul tie in place even after it has been renounced. This really hurts a lot, I know but it is crucially important. It is almost the same as holding on to the dead in a negative way, by keeping remnants of the dead we are negatively clinging on the dead and refusing to say goodbye which is the same principle with holding onto objects and gifts of past partners which leaves open doors to entities and forces unknown because we never know what the persons carry with them. Simply put the longer we hold on the longer we delay our own progress and automatically become the demon in the story of the person we lock in our hearts by keeping such remnants or belongings of sentimental value.

Step #6 Renounce and break the soul tie in Jesus' name

Finally, you need to **verbalize a prayer to break off the soul ties**. You need to speak it out! Life and death are in the power of the tongue so when you speak out you are declaring with your mouth the power of Christ to break the ties to your past. Verbally renouncing something carries a lot of weight in the spiritual realm. Just as vows can bind the soul, renouncing can release the soul from bonds. Jesus said that whatsoever you shall loose will be loosed in heaven (the heavenly realm, or spiritual realm). You can renounce and loose yourself from an ungodly soul tie by simply speaking something like this from your heart:

Here is an Illustration to help you understand the concept of successfully breaking soul tie in Jesus Might Name.

"I now renounce and loose myself from any ungodly soul ties formed between myself and (mention the persons by

Name)__________, and I break these ungodly soul ties in Jesus' name."

5 Signs of Success

Sign #1 The first thing that will come to your mind and spirit is the fact that fornication wasted your time, money and life, especially for those under and who were operating in lust to the last degree which is beyond the word perversion, I thank God I never reached that level. The last level is where men and women can no longer control their sexual urges and rape becomes normal as well as bestiality. You reach the point where you cannot even think of sex anymore, seeing sex, anything porn related your spirit cannot even tolerate such rubbish. Your thinking becomes clear, your life becomes peaceful.

Sign #2 if you were are a man or women of God you now have clarity back and God begins to restore you to your former glory, your gifting's and ministry excel beyond imagination. In my case, the Anointing was drained and I realized I stopped seeing visions, and dreaming became less often which were replaced by seriously terrifying nightmares.

Sign #3 you are now able to see the opposite sex for what they are not meat bags. You see a mind body and spirit that makes them human. Rapists and sex traffickers do not see the opposite sex as human beings. Fornication & Lust work hand in hand.

Sign #4 Freedom from the slavery of sex and lustful desires. You are in full control of your manhood/genital organs. You no longer need pornography and vibrators are a big No as well as masturbation of any kind. You are FREE in JESUS Name.

Sign #5 Success comes naturally to you where you were constantly failing in the past. Lastly you will feel sick as soul ties are broken; symptoms like malaria will be experienced. A strange taste in your mouth, a strange smell and weakness in your spirit as something powerful is happening inside. This may not be the same case for everyone so no need to doubt, at this point if you do not experience these signs it is okay.

I purposely left out the obvious thing to note. Once a soul tie is broken you are no longer connected to that person hence, the addictive craving, that maddening sensation of being needed or suffocating, the feeling of; "I can't live my life without you is broken for good." Life goes on smoothly effortlessly and painless, you can picture the person with another lover and have peace of mind. Is not God good?

CHAPTER FIVE

Four signs you are in a bad relationship

Warnings from Friends & Family;

This first sign is highly unnoticed but very crucial. The reason for this is that this warning is one that is supernatural and comes to the **Victim** in *Four Main Stages;* the first sign is from a **Parent Figure**. The Parent can be anyone from biological mom and dad to mom and dad's brothers or sisters. The Second Sign comes from an Elderly person who bonds (Soul-Tie) with you by your decision to look up to that person as a Parent Figure who is not biologically related to you in any way. The elderly person who gave me advice by these words; "you shouldn't date." Three very simple words that seemed cruel at the time when spoken but today are clearly understood and I am very thankful. I wondered a lot why she would say that and

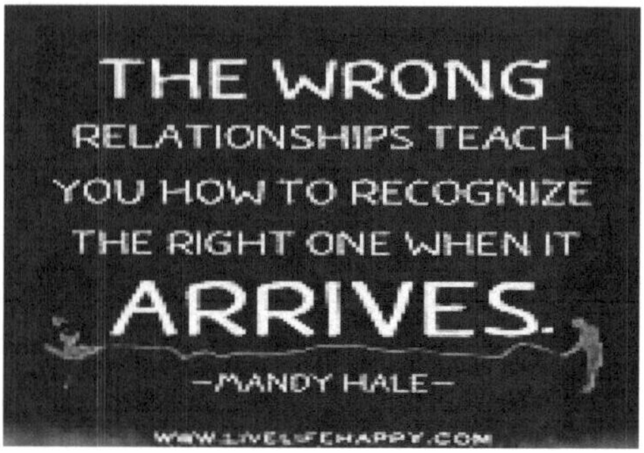

naturally went into my feelings often. To me the most logical explanation was that she very well knew my history with an ex who I had cheated on and critically.

Broke the poor girl's heart, but that was not the case. The third sign comes from your **Siblings & Cousins,** theywarn you *expressly* even in great detail, in fact they beckon you not to date and even go the extra mile showing you why you should leave but you just don't listen. The last being the fourth sign comes from your **Closest of Friend's.** These are the ones you can count on for anything even though they hardly in your personal space but the moment you say "bro's lets chill" I assure you they will enjoy your company until you tell them to leave and when they are leaving the goodbye is an intimate moment be it male or female.

To understand why good relationships end and one of the reasons are **jealous friends with black hearts.** Eve and I were a very happy couple up until I started noticing this pain in her heart, she would change from time to time and the hurting was so much that it would also affect me. That is how close we became. What would hurt the other, what would upset the other; the both of us felt it. We loved each other truly. The pain she was hiding from me would almost send her in tears I remember being strong enough to only ask her once, what is wrong? Nothing she replied, while deep down I knew something is chewing away her happiness and that she was not comfortable speaking to me about it. My failure-to-ensure-communication between us was my gravest mistake that cost our very sacred happiness.

I remember being so connected to the point both our hearts and souls were in accord. In fact, the very day that she broke up with me I knew it would happen as I felt her beating heart make no sound but silence as it stood still with the song "Goodbye My Lover" by James Blunt playing in my head. I knew our love was over and I also knew not to fight or resist it; but all I wanted to know was the reason why we ended? Off which she never ever disclosed, and that hurt for the longest time as it never made moving on any easier. Every time goodbye my lover or Tattoo by Jordin Sparks aired or played on the television I would find myself breaking in despair wondering why? What have I done wrong and could it be fixed?

Once I realized sulking and poking at her to tell me what had happened for the sudden decision would not solve anything, I decided to man up and play detective and to my surprise I had a bounty hunter on my head reporting every single move I made back to her from my class time to my lunch time. She knew my entire circle. Now most gurus out there state that a girl that monitors you is cheating but that is not accurately true. Eve was not and is not the cheating kind, I knew her to well.

Some girls are just naturally jealous like that but in Eve's case she was told that I was cheating on her which was not true. I was still an innocent Nice-Guy with my virginity attached safely. Eve simply was processing gossip that was not entirely false as the justification for my cheating lies in the fact that she was told my entire family, the males are bad people and all of them are cheaters by nature. Eve decided to believe her fanatic Christian friends over her nice guy who truly loved her like no other.

Once my detective skills came to full use it had been five years of grieving over her. My heart was content inknowing

That she never left because I was the problem or that I never treated her well. I was simply out for the truth and I got it. That is what helped me move on. Going back to the forms that make up a relationship, lies kill a relationship that is why I ventured for the truth. The worst thing to do to your partner is end the relationship with no justifiable reason.

Never just end anything with silence, by doing so you are opening up that person to the poisonous whispers of the devil, where nothing but pain and torment await the person. We all know that silence is deadly as it is the worst form of ignoring someone. Imagine a son asking a father or a mother for food and both parents remain silent pretending as if the child never even spoke in the first place. Now imagine the child's confused feelings of rejection, feelings of isolation. Now imagine you were that child. What would you do and what would be your reaction? In the end, you can never escape the "Jealous-Friends".

No matter where you turn to or whom you are dating, they will always interfere with your love life. They come as your friend but behind your back, they are gossiping and backbiting about you, feeding poisonous lies to your lover just to ruin and destroy your happiness. We must remember that not all people can enter a successful relationship as not all have what it takes. Some people have not yet healed, they are torn up, they are hurting, grieving and are not yet one with themselves. Many are still working on self-discovery as they are trying to find out who they are and what they life purpose is. Others are extremely unhappy with life for various reasons but move around portraying a fictitious smile that needs discernment to see through the lie.

For all the reasons mentioned in the above paragraph, most people enter into a relationship based on various lies and as a result, these are one of the many reasons that many.

Relationships end prematurely with no hope of ever lasting longer than six-months. With such types of relationships, most people know that they are no good but stubbornly start dating just to make a year or more to achieve their selfish ambition. The youth in this generation really need to sit down and evaluate what exactly is and makes up a successful relationship rather than just sleeping around with partner after partner increasing the chances of attracting the deadly virus as well as sexually transmitted diseases and not forgetting early and unwanted pregnancies.

A relationship is not a Toy or a Barbie Doll but rather an intimate gift of sharing love and affection between two separate individuals being man and female. Anything outside of this context does not sum up a relationship. Furthermore, a successful relationship needs both the couple not to forget their life goals as most people once settled forget about their individual lives and sacrifice almost all their time together by putting a hold to their lives for one another. If you are in a relationship or soon decide to enter one always remember that your life should never be put on hold for the sake of love otherwise that is not a relationship but damnation of your souls.

In my case, for example I discovered that the second girl to start a relationship with was not productive enough because we were always fighting rather than sitting down and planning the future. We sat all day and night talking but never really discussing; and when we did decide to talk, it was over petty things and petty fights whereby I needed to be the one always saying baby I'm sorry.

I loved too much and that again ladies and gentleman is a very big problem. In this world of dating, it is the female who must first fall in love with the male and then the male swiftly follows suit. A vice-versa scenario almost never works and the female either flees or in my case becomes stupid and pumped with pride thinking that I will never get another girl just like her. Woman allow me to tell you, "There are plenty fish in the sea;" so never get hyped with this kind of pride, its ugly and no man will gladly tolerate it.

There are some things that are intellectually common for both male and female to simply not do. No one wants to be called boring so do not use mean words on your partner. No one wants to be bullied or abused in a relationship. We come together to complete each other and not to fight each other. Arguments here and there are healthy but not every single day. Be productive by building one another especially where the word of God isconcerned.

In this case, the warnings are from the good will of all Four Figures and this is why. Man is made or consists of or is a Trinity, Three in one however, you like to see it, Body Spirit and Soul (Mind). At this stage it is within the Spirit that the warnings come from, as the spirit according to the Bible in the **Book of 1 Corinthian's Chapter 12 Verses 10-11** with the following writings; " to another the working of miracles, to another prophecy, to another discerning of spirits, to another different kinds of tongues, to another the interpretation of tongues. 11 But one and the same Spirit works all these things, distributing to each one individually as He wills."

Looking at the underlined portion *discerning of spirits,* the spiritual ability or gift given by **Gods Holy Spirit** to men to able to notice what kind of spirits people carry or feel or even see demons at a later stage of the gift being enhanced through daily prayer and walking with God. Now to clarify the warnings; come as a way to spare you from entering or continuing a negative or bad relationship which will by all means break you, affect your life, lead to failure etc. the list goes on. Please understand it's not that all warnings implore that the man or women carry evil spirits sometimes it's baggage from unhealed past relationships and many other things unseen by the naked eyes. In the end people miss out on these warnings thinking we know better than our parents, elders, family and friends when in actual fact they are only looking out for you and wish you the best in life. So rather than feel humiliated that they were right in the end, turn to them and thank them for giving you advice and apologies for not at the time being able to receive their good will.

An Unexpected Sudden Change of Character;
I know thousands have been there, a very unpleasant experience where you give out your heart and soul at a rate of 100% thinking yes I have finally won the Lottery. The first version of this book series looks into this concept of giving yourself entirely, which is wrong for men. To be honest first the woman must open up before the man does. Gentlemen, remember its Ladies first at all times. So here you are you bump in or meet this girl and or guy saying to yourself if only I could have that fine peace of meat I'd be good singing in your heart Kid Cudi - Pursuit of Happiness, then to your surprise your wish gets granted and the next minute you're in the heat of romance everyone singing love birds and complementing how good you are together, however none of these are your actual friends just outside sources. The first few months are very smooth you even start daydreaming, this must be Heaven? Smiling nonstop life is good to you. Everything you most probably wanted in the person is there and then the ***Mental Trauma*** happens. From nowhere your partner reveals this very dark side that somehow just resents you and sees nothing good in you at all. Let's remember that the physical and supernatural

are a double sided coin spinning at the same time but the only reason we are unable to perceive the supernatural with our physical senses is mainly because both worlds have a difference in time more like time zones. In the spirit-world things happen at the speed of light so in other words the physical world is much slower in movement. For one to prophecy by the voice of God or even see a vision it happens in the mind for a few seconds such as having a trance whereby a person falls asleep for a short period of time but when he interprets what he saw the timing simply does not match up.

The same case with near death experiences, a person who may have been on the brink of death for under a period of five good minutes when revived speaks for about an hour or more on what his spirit perceived when he traveled through the doorway to the other side of life. This is the concept that is applied to the change of character remember evil spirits can exist in a person without the naked eye noticing. I am now talking about those petty fights where very nasty words were spoken that left a mark/wound that is unhealed today. Some of these words carry a demonic power that leaves the victim depressed or even paralyzed as the evil words were enacted by the entity on purpose with the sole purpose of binding, freezing, destroying, breaking, and diminishing the person's character or life. For example if you are a writer, a poet, a singer, a movie star whether you are in it or aspiring to be one, these words carry power to destroy your hopes and dreams hence, some people give in and do just that, they break and give up, they end the relationship carrying broken egos and corrupted minds. Leaving no space for healing the two became one and so we hear of cases where the person changed and now carries the same character damaging other poor souls.

Negative Feelings:

Now that you are one flesh, whether you are dating or finally decided to call it quits, you have what is called emotional baggage from previous relationships. In other words; you become just like your partner. At this stage you are lost and trying to find a balance in your life, as you have lost focus on your hopes and dreams, and all sense of who you are as an individual since you have become **One Flesh** i.e. Your thinking is not off your own but your partners and whatever spirits you both carry. This stage of life is very crucial and if left unchecked can result to death. This is the stage where soul ties are at its highest peak.

What we further need to understand is that whenever we have sex especially unholy sex by that I mean sex outside marriage there are evil spirits that watch as you violate God's laws. These are things you will not hear or read in church to the fullest degree as its too indecent to talk about and further than this people do not want to hear about demons and the dangers of sex because we live in a world that is too cool for God and His standards; so we would rather water down the instructions of God which are good and save us from destruction to fit in with the world and enjoy the pleasures it has to offer.

The reason woman are depicted as destiny killers is not because God is bias but the Devil knows very well how easy it is to use a woman to destroy a man hence, Eve destroyed Adams legacy shortly after listening to the Devil. Ask yourselves why didn't the Devil go directly to Adam? There is a power a woman carries and Satan knows how best to exploit it without the woman realizing what is happening. I mean woman are smart but not spiritually smart. Do you really think Eve was not aware of the command of God not to eat the forbidden fruit? The same way the Devil got to

Eve is the same way he influences many women worldwide to lead men into sin. We look into later.

Negative feelings in this cycle is the process explained by Kris whereby you feel you are being watched even though you are far away from your partner. Remember your thoughts are not your own and yes you are being watched by the spirits you bound yourself to. These evils watch over you in jealousy to ensure you're not happy by that, they get angry when you talk to the opposite sex hence, that negative energy you feel is their mark on your flesh that you belong to them. I will expand on these evils shortly.

Coming this far I congratulate you and assure you that healing is coming your way as we get into the reasons why Men Cheat later on. As the both of you are one flesh your thoughts become one and this only means the ***mental trauma*** will only get worse most especially if both of you are highly spiritual persons by that I mean walk with God daily. There was a time when I could not conceal my thoughts of wanting to end the relationship from an ex. We could be in the same room either chatting or watching a movie and the moment I began to reflect on how bad we had gotten and think off the best way to pull out without hurting her, she would snap and tell me to just leave, as she would get in her feelings and cry I realized then this won't be easy! As she expressed all that she said so too would the Evil Spirits speak the most evil and harsh words through her mouth. Many times when she calmed down she would bitterly cry apologizing stating she was not the one speaking asking me to help her. When you are in this state of mind (mixed emotions), your focus is maximized beyond a 100% in trying to resolve what's broken which is dangerous because you are now tampering with the supernatural forces not fully documented. At this stage the best advice I have for you, Is too; '*Flee like Joseph.*" There is no fixing anything at this stage it only gets worse, even prayers are not enough. I have had my fair share in casting out demons and gloried in the power of God but the great Evil responsible for my decision to not engage in any affair until I fully heal showed me how much time I wasted and how much power it drained from my life.

Abortions & miscarriages:

To conclude on the above three points, Jealousy wait I mean abnormal jealousy is a great sign of an unhealthy relationship. We all know the saying, *"too much is poisonous."* In this case hazardous as no peace of mind exists and you are constricted to one place not by choice. When both couples start questioning loyalty something very sick is happening. Flee! Nothing good is coming your way. Do not be deluded in change when these four signs are at your door.

The Fourth and final sign; Abortions (Crimes too vile to be shared with the World at Large) these are the very serious, very negative effects of a good relationship gone wrong. This is the Devils doing, Satan's end game as seen in Romans 8:6-8 "For the mind set on the flesh is death, but the mind set on the Spirit is life and peace, because the mind set on the flesh is hostile toward God; for it does not subject itself to the law of God, for it is not even able to do so; and those who are in the flesh cannot please God."

Abortions happen as a result of a couple not breaking the relationship at stage three. Now that all that negativity and hate is built up along with a change in intimacy, as sex is no longer the same but rather strange and foreign and often the only way of expressing the unhealthy feelings the flesh and the mind are not in sink resulting to failure in timing the release of pleasure. At this point, no one really cares about each other so the relationship becomes very dangerous. There's this show called Crimes of Passion, you would be amazed how violent relationships become. At this point both partners have the intension to cheat just to hurt the other, the romance dies out and turns to vengeance.

There is this young couple that went through all these stages without even realizing what was happening to them. The women with a knife removed his genitals and very interestingly the man was stitched up, survived and went to jail for cheating, imagine that. The fact is many couples go through these phases and might not ever have a clue unless they humble themselves and seek the rightful help that they need. Council and therapy can help I don't deny because casting out demons involves council and therapy but goes beyond that by cancelling evil spirits and removing baggage via divine healing which has only started being understood now. If you are in this mess and need healing there is hope for you, absolutely nothing to worry about.

This is my poem on abortion:

One minute you happy and the next everything goes to Hell. You sit and ponder looking for the joyous memories and yet find none but misery and pain as hard as you look for the good, all you see is bad. Voices echoing so loud, you try to ignore them but you just can't. They only get louder by day screaming, "Murderer;" painting a bloody scenario with your hands, you see so vividly, pictures of blood stained hands, as red as scarlet you wonder why. Full of questions as your heart echoes what wrong have I done to deserve this. Torment and depression constantly knocking at your door, louder and louder the thud in your head, voices yelling "Murderer." Many sleepless nights pass you by as Depression and misery are now your comforters, Insomnia is the one who welcomes the Devil, after all Death was the first to be invited and now you lost in a maze wondering what next with your life, where did I go wrong? It's almost like a dream, please someone wake me up. Stop pinching yourself before you get hurt, there is hope for you. A time will come, you will smile again; I promise. -R.P

How to be forgiven for this Grave Sin?

The Secret of forgiveness from abortion is to confess this heavy sin as murder because that is what abortion is, whether it was a week old in the womb your act took an innocent life which God detests. The doctrine of sin is another error the church does not yet understand, look at this clearly. Sins differ with sever magnitude and the 7 deadly sins are what breaks our relationship with God i.e. automatic disqualification from Gods Holy Presence just like Adam & Eve.

The Seven Deadly Sins

Proverbs 6:16-19 records the seven sins that God considers as detestable. Here is the list where He says, "There are six things the Lord hates, seven that are detestable to him." 1) Feet Eager to run to Evil. 2) A lying witness who gives false testimony. 3) One who stirs up trouble among brothers (Slander).4) Arrogant Eyes. 5) A lying Tongue. 6) Hands that shed innocent Blood (Murderers). 7) A heart that plots wicked schemes (Iniquity).

CHAPTER SIX

Alpha Males: The reason I grew up a cheat

There is this Stigma towards cheaters surrounded by a saying; "once a cheat, always a cheat." This is highly not always the case as I stand to be a reformed cheater by the love of God and by His Power I am free from the manipulation of lust. You see the thing is right after experiencing the pain for myself I knew then what I know now, cheating is not just very hurtful but very wrong, its sick and twisted I dare say. It not only affects the couple but others around you. A change in one relationship may result to catastrophe in other relationships such as your friends and family that like or even love your partner. I realized It's better to cut it while in fornication stage before it grows with me towards and even into Adultery stage in which case I'm certain would be beyond the word catastrophe itself. After tasting cheating at fornication level I can only imagine how messed up cheating is at Adultery level, I mean what about the poor children and that's how it all began for me, let's take a trip down memory lane.

As a young boy with older cousins and friends who I looked up to as Alpha Males, these guys are legends I mean they could change women every single month literally. No names mentioned so bear with me. I was always amazed at how they did it, I mean they were legends but when it came to my uncles they were stars; laughing aloud, until today they do not want to burn out. What am I saying? Ok let me clarify, as a child watching and studying and questioning these individuals who seemed to have something I knew I never had and could not describe it till date the only word for these beings is *''Alpha Male."* To be honest I admired them, one of the best cousins who I really found interesting was from another city, Lilongwe so I only got to see him once in a while as I was in Blantyre for most of my childhood.

I remember this one time we spent summer holiday together, one of my best times. I learned a lot about women and if remember very well, the second time we were together again I already had two girlfriends maybe even more. To be honest, I do not even remember, until today I get calls why did you cheat on me as well as texts very disturbing in nature as I really do not remember so I ask myself was I really all that bad or are some of these babes faking it. What am I trying to say now, ok let us get straight to it? I believe there are two main reasons as to why men cheat and the rest follow afterwards. Are you ready for the hard truth?

I am giving you three memories, the first being the time my phone rang while my cousin was with his wife in the car. Yes please take note my cousin is married until date. At the time of the call I was in the shower, had just finished drying myself. We had this routine whenever he was going to work he would drop me off at my uncles place, simply because his wife never liked me a real weird woman. After work, he would come for me then together return home. That morning when my phone rang and I had missed it and while I was dressing he shouted out loud, "Admar your girlfriend just called," this was my reply; "which one?" his wife gave me this very strange look but I never understood it till today as I'm free from reason number two as to why men cheat. My cousin too was perplexed and called me aside to observe me and give a hint of my mistake which I never understood either way, these were his words, " Never say which one next time just tell me thanks and tell her ill call her back or something sweet." I simply understood the sweet and flattery words not the aspect of immorality.

Later that evening he took me places, three separate hot babes' homes to be frank, I swear all these women were just fine foxes if I describe any more detail women will have a problem with me so let us just picture angels here right. Now look at this I never felt not even a little remorse or the energy to tell his wife you are being cheated on laughing aloud, poor woman. I remember when they would fight over her insecurities and text messages but he was too smart for her. Her way of showing her anger was petty things like not cooking for us and gossiping about me, any way it never worked reasons too deep for this platform.

This is my cousins life now let us go to my uncles. The last born has about 18 kids with different woman, I once called him when I was having doubts and asked him how do you do it. He told me *"the secret is simple, just lie."* I could not wait to implement it. I approached this angel in church on a Sunday afternoon when during a party where I saw with my own innocent eyes one of the members being female urinate in her pants after getting drunk. To be honest I just remembered that now as my mind closed it for being very disturbing. Anyhow, this was a catholic church laughing aloud. So there I was and my eyes caught the attention of this angel who I approached and engaged in conversation. After about 30 minutes of innocent talk and church things, I remembered my uncle's words and like a pro, I released lies and the next 30 minutes I was at my place and later an hour away from her home this became our Sunday routine and about three Sundays later we were dating.

Going back to my uncles and one more who I cannot mention. There came a time when I was around 16 I got a call from the one I cannot mention to meet him outside. I was home at the time of this very disturbing scene. There I was thinking what could be this urgent. Making my way outside I find the car with the lights turned off and a hand is waving calling me to the window. Upon arrival, I see the one I cannot mention and then I see the other two and then I see three strange and unfamiliar faces; they were prostitutes. Confused very confused I look at all of them wondering why the Hell! They had called me in the first place. They reactions as calm as possible nothing wrong at all in their faces. So I registered this is normal. You will not believe what they had asked me, *"Admar do you have condoms?"* Perplexed I answered no and went back inside as though nothing had happened. My granny asks me what he wanted. Nothing important I said and life went on.

I remember when the one I cannot mention had an argument with his women on two accounts for two reasons. The first one was when will you marry me she exhaled, followed by I know you do not want to marry me, I also know you prefer to sleep with prostitutes than myself. He looked at me feeling a little bit of shame just a little bit but not too much. Why am I bringing about all these memories?

Two main reasons men cheat:

REASON (1) the first and most important reason why men cheat is the way the manner they been *raised*. By that, I mean the kind of people that surrounded them from birth. A very famous Psychotherapist known as **Mr. Gary Neuman;** who wrote in his book- *the truth about cheating*; agrees with me on this point. In his research, it is not number one reason, however his survey conveys the following results being, **200%** of the men who admitted to being unfaithful towards their partners. **48%** gave the reason for cheating being "*emotional dissatisfaction*" because men seek praise & Admiration, **40%** find this praise from their colleagues, **88%** cheated with women less attractive than their partners and **77%** were enablers hence, close friendships with other cheaters and only **68%** felt guilty about cheating.

REASON (2) the second reason is plain and simple lust, which can take first place interchangeably. As men seek praise and admiration from the world both male and female, we want our ego's felt all around us. To be honest nothing feeds a man's ego like cheating. As funny as that sounds especially to women allow me to clarify why I say so. In the mind of an Alpha, his ability to engage with various women at the same time as being in a relationship or marriage is not wrong but male power and they have this thing in them that they are good at what they do and this leads to other males complementing hence even men may praise other man. In the end cheating for men becomes inherent, a mental cycle that needs to be broken. I will clarify on this second reason being lust in the detail shortly.

CHAPTER SEVEN

The Beast & Cycle that needs to be broken

Romans 13:14 «But put on the Lord Jesus Christ, and make no provision for the flesh in regard to its lusts.»

As long as you are occupied in doing God's will, the flesh does not have opportunity to sin. It is when we become idle and our minds become idle that our flesh begins to drift toward its natural inclination to sin.

A man's spirit and flesh (body) are at constant war with each other as the spirit desires to cling onto God and things that are just, good and holy while the body desperately chases after immoral things and carnality of this world. To put it simple lust has levels before it grows and what the world never knew is that both male and female are subject to lust in the same way with one small difference, the events of a woman falling into lust the way a man does is quite rare and that is why the world is unaware that women too are lustful. This topic was dealtwith in why women cheat.

The Stages of Lust:

1 Hunger for carnality-

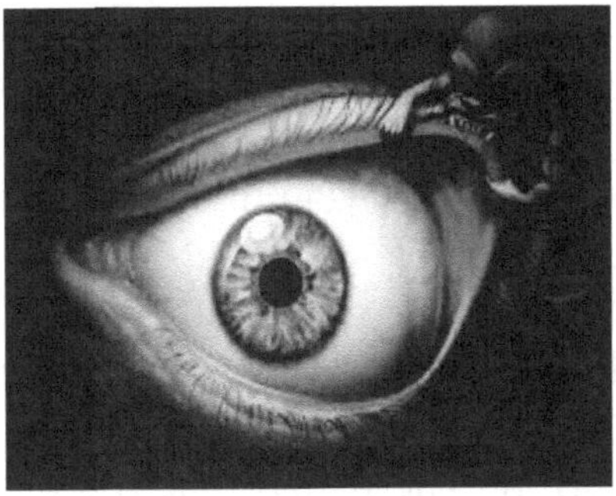

Once puberty has taken its toll on your body that is ages 12 to 16 the era of experiencing and finding out what you are made off this is the stage that takes away most people's innocence especially women as "women mature way faster than men." Men please do not misunderstand; by the time, you had your first sexual experience a woman most likely has triple the experience. Just to show you what I mean, the first time you get intimate with a women you go easy on her for the sake of her modesty thinking the only position she knows is missionary. What you will find as intimacy advances she then takes the lead by asking you if you have ever tried doggy or other positions when all along she already knows what she is doing.

After puberty, the hormones are on fire for carnal knowledge. This hunger cannot be helped it is like a blood rush for the taste of blood if you could be a vampire.

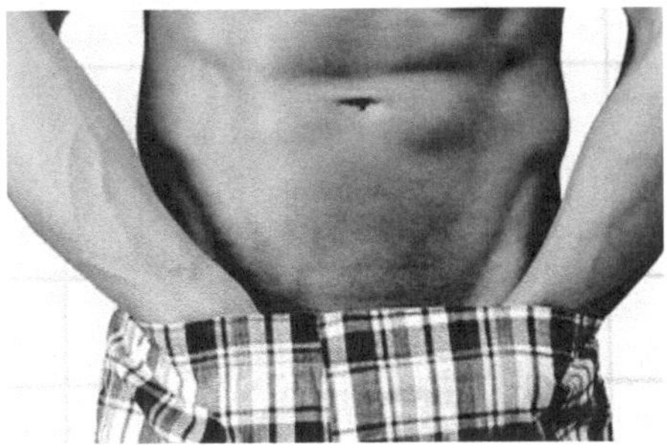

This is the first stage where the flesh starts to wage war over your spirit. At this point, you are innocent and all you want is to obey your flesh by giving it what it wants, which is not as easy as it feels.

2 Masturbation- The second stage. To be honest a cousin of mine taught me how to masturbate. I learnt that men teach each other I have no idea about women but I would like to know someday. At this stage, you learn to play with yourself. As the playing goes on so does your innocence and purity leaving you open or vulnerable to the supernatural. Most people who did it the first time successfully received carnal knowledge instantly and knew at the moment that such activity is wrong. Guilt and shame instantly awakens a feeling you never knew before. The second time you did it I'm sure you don't remember but what is certain is the fact that each time you played with yourself you did it in secret and over time explored for more satisfaction. At this point of receiving/registering carnal knowledge, I bet the feeling was the same as Adam & Eve who sinned and hid themselves from the face and presence of God. In this case, of awakened carnal knowledge your parents/guardians were in the position of God in your life in whom you hid yourself.

3 Pornography- The third stage. As you masturbated seeking new and much more exciting sexual experiences, you came to a point where your body wanted more than you were giving it. Somewhere in your carnal knowledge, it clicked that your private part is and or was designed to enter the vagina and vice-versa for women. Mysteriously someone randomly shows up to meet

your need or feed your flesh what it needs to know. You are then introduced to pornography and your masturbation life kicks off to **level two** where by your flesh and soul are engaged in sexual arousal. The more you watched pornography and consciously and or even subconsciously registered all the moves and positions from how to hold the man/ woman your body was even more hungry and desired much more than you were feeding it thus, pornography got old and carnally you knew the purpose of your penis/vagina.

4 Fornication- Level three. The stage most people lose their souls (mind) as they cannot control themselves right after their very first time. To be honest I have seen both male and female lives ruined after losing their virginity, which is the third level of carnality that unlocks beyond sexual arousal, as now all three levels are open mind, body and spirit connection as discussed above (Soul-Ties).

Lust is Born- The fourth and final level. Lust is a spirit, which ripens to possess/enter/use a person's sexual appetite immorally. From this point on some people are not satisfied with the same sex and go after the opposite sex. Some are still not satisfied and go after animals, which is called, bestiality hence both male and females sleep with all types of animals and in modern day bestiality, exist porn hubs just like gay porn is accessible on the internet.

New International Version

Romans 1:26-28

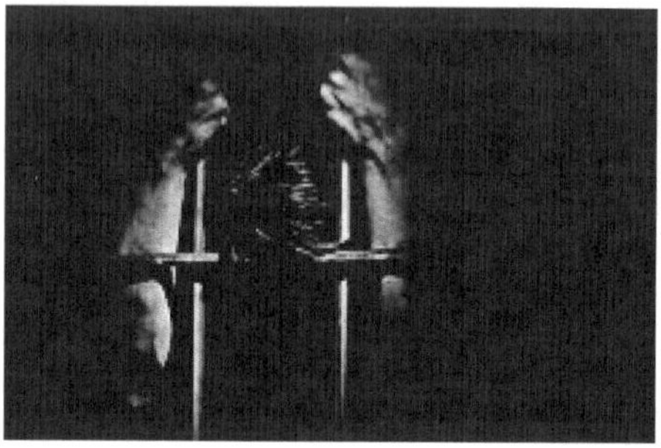

"Because of this, God gave them over to shameful lusts. Even their women exchanged natural sexual relations for unnatural ones. In the same way the men also abandoned natural relations with women and were inflamed with lust for one another. Men committed shameful acts with other men, and received in themselves the due penalty for their error. **28** Furthermore, just as they did not think it worthwhile to retain the knowledge of God, so God gave them over to a depraved mind, so that they do what ought not to be done."

In the end as much as science wants to blame homosexuality on genes malfunction such is a pure lie with no truth in it. I tell you no man or woman is born gay because no man/ women is born with lust unless the spirit enters the child at birth, which is very rare. The only evil spirits that follow bloodlines are Ancestral Spirits, which are not sexual spirits hence; there is no spiritual explanation for homosexuality except when the spirit of lust who only moves in when carnal knowledge is ripe for the taking.

To conclude on homosexuality, the disease is passed on through intercourse at an early age being the first stage of carnal knowledge whereby in the process of experiencing; lust may maliciously move in and take advantage of children both male and female to sexually engage with one another. The more they explore the more they like it and the usual happens, the more you practice one thing the better you become at it which, in this case becomes normal and life goes on. Children grew up homosexual; they are not born gay. The Spirit of Lust may be passed on during these immoral activities. Thereby taking control of the person and body. I once interviewed a couple of homosexuals and this is what I discovered.

One boy the age of 8-years was violently and sexually abused. He was rapped by an elderly gardener after school hours, his anus was ripped and the bleeding was heavy. He was given 28 stitches and after healing which took months from both physical and mental trauma he explained something clicked in his head and it all made sense. Today he is one of the biggest gays I know. We argued once over the subject I saw the spirit manifest in his anger against me. I know very well he does not like me. The thing that clicked was possession nothing more. The gardener was old and the spirit was done with a faded body. The spirit was starving in other words and found no use in the old man so it jumped into the 8-year-old boy who then grew up gay and far from God.

Childhood traumas affect many people until date. You would be surprised the number of very sad and disturbing cases that both man and women open up concerning their past lives. We need to protect our children from what they see and hear. Bible says; *"what you see and hear you become."* Children exposed to filth at a young age become very troubled in life and meet many problems one way or the other; their lives are ruined from the start of bad parenting. Names are also very important, this goes to African parents, please the names you give your kids carry a blessing or a curse, strength or weakness. Too be honest some names are just ugly and yet we all have African roots.

It is interesting how the Media is trying to brainwash us by portraying homosexual relationships on movies and series.

It is clear that the next generations will have the excuse to claim they were born gay. Any way I am not against gays because the bible is not against them. God only gave up on them and allowed them to give into their desires so nowhere do I say pick up stones and kill them. They are human beings just like us and you will not find anywhere in the bible any single verse that condemns them to death. Every person that has raised up a hand in killing any single person who is gay is guilty of bloodshed and will be judged on the day of reckoning. You are evil and have a murderous spirit who are you to put words in Gods mouth?

I only speak on what God has spoken in His word. These are the stages that open a man or women up to the supernatural. I shall be shedding more light on this subject in regards to the two main reasons why men cheat and show just how all other reasons follow suit. To conclude on this chapter, the main reason a man cheats is **the way a man is raised and the** second reason, which follows suit, is the **degree of lust in a man.** In the next chapter I will get into detail and elaborate in full why men cheat.

CHAPTER EIGHT

A man that shows emotion is a good man

While it is true that a man who shows emotion is a good man, a man that cries is no different from a woman. Any other crying except crying when in the Lord Jesus Presence, that man is no different to a woman; such a man is subject to gossip. A man strongly attached to his emotions is a strong man while a man who is prone to tears is a weak man. Two questions, is gossip bad? Moreover, what is it in the first place? Gossip has a ***religious*** stigma attached to it so in order to understand it we need to look at three things

(Religion, Society & Psychology).

Oxford dictionary defines Gossip as follows, "casual or unconstrained conversation or reports about other people, typically involving details which are not confirmed as

true." Now to expand this definition and consolidate the meaning we can look into Society through the lenses of science under the study of **Unolifo Research** which found that, men use more grey matter compared to women who use more white matter compared to men. Long story short white matter gives women the ability to multi task, think better emotionally and process information better than man, which makes women better communicators than men hence, when there is a problem women resort to talking things through while men prefer to use their fists which is something women will never understand.

Psychology on the one hand holds that gossip is the "Standard currency of human connection." Which means there is nothing wrong with gossip as it is nothing but a means of communicating something that women do and love. In other words, women can never stop gossiping, as it is their very nature to gossip. From the Dictionary of *Oxford,* we denote the existence of two types of gossip which are "casual & unconstrained," Which means it is possible to gossip (communicate with others) without trashing someone else's name/reputation which by law is a crime and known as Defamation whereby, the things spoken are untrue and the strongest defense against such a crime in the Court of Law is the nothing but the purest Truth.

Gossip under the religious stigma, can just as well be easily explained. The problem with the stigma is misinterpretation of the *Holy Words of God.* Let us examine a few scriptures starting with the book of proverbs that is also known as, the book of wisdom.

Using the Original authority **King James Bible, Proverbs 20:19** "He that goeth about as a talebearer revealeth secrets: therefore meddle not with him that flattereth with his lips." Now just to show you how ridiculous modern translations are have a Look at this **New Living Translation** "A gossip goes around telling secrets, so do not hang around with chatterers." The bible is clear; Gossip is not wrong when it is casual communication but when *gossip* becomes *slander*! There is a problem. Look at **King James Bible Proverbs 16:28** "a froward (**NKJV** Perverse) man soweth strife: and whisperer separateth chief friends." Other versions say a perverse/troublemaker etc. New Living Translation "A troublemaker plants seeds of strife; gossip separates the best of friends." In short a person who speaks evil, vile, bad of another person to get his way over the other person is perverse/troublemaker and will be punished according to **Exodus 20:16 King James Bible** "Thou shalt not bear false witness against thy neighbour." **New International Version** "You shall not give false testimony against your neighbor." Bear in mind this is one of the **10 commandments.**

Once again, there is nothing wrong with gossip but when gossip becomes perverse then it becomes a sin. New International Version

"A gossip betrays a confidence, but a trustworthy person keeps a secret." This Bible Verse is clear and self-explanatory. This leaves one last question, why do women gossip so much? According to a study by **Edward Burns**, the psychology of women tells us that they; "are driven by deep sexual and primitive competitive urges," which clearly explains a lot pertaining to the fact that women have difficulties getting along.

Now not everybody you tell ***"do not tell anyone/Not A SOUL"*** is a betrayer, there is a temptation that comes upon hearing that sentence which cannot be explained. Jesus understood it very well after He would heal/help/cast out a demon He said make sure *to tell no one* but few minutes later the word is out. My point is a true friend knows how and when to keep a secret but even a true friend will be tempted to speak if you tell him/her "do not tell anyone" as this sentence is a public and political tool used to send a message secretively.

If I'm to bring back **Mr. Gary Neuman's** survey to illustrate and expand the reasons as to why men cheat from my main two reasons which are understood from a spiritual point of view in the context, *"what a man sees he becomes."*

In his book- ***the truth about cheating***; he agrees with me on this point however, in his research it is not number one reason holding the following result's being, **200%** of the men who admitted to being unfaithful towards their partners, **48%** gave the reason for cheating being *"emotional dissatisfaction"* because men seek praise & Admiration, **40%** find this praise from their colleagues, **88%** cheated with women less attractive than their partners and **77%** were enablers hence, close friendships with other cheaters and only **68%** felt guilty about cheating.

If we pay close attention to the results of the survey, we will notice that the two highest figures are 88% being cheaters who slept with women less attractive to their actual partners and the second highest number at 77% being enablers we can derive four reasons men cheat on their women by looking into the psychology of men. With my main two reasons we have four reasons but before we get into it let us examine common and unrealistic reasons from a female perspective to further note more and acceptable reasons.

According the blog by ***Life Advancer*** she has **8** reasons which I would like to evaluate in regards to a common pattern that rhymes with tones of other research so here goes, her **8 reasons why men cheat the women they love.**

1. Men cheat because they are immature.

"Men often lack the maturity to fully understand that their infidelity is nearly always discovered eventually and it will inevitably have devastating consequences like hurting their partners, families and that they might even lose the women they love."

2. Men cheat because they are insecure.

"He might feel that he is too old or too young, not smart enough, not handsome enough, etc. to be desired. He chooses infidelity to get validation from other women, to feel better about himself and to feel that he is worthy, desirable, and attractive to others."

3. Men cheat because they want to save their marriages.

"Many men cannot be called good communicators. When they have problems with their partners and do not know how to fix them, they think it is much better to look for comfort elsewhere. They may feel trapped and unhappy in their relationships but they do not want to hurt their partners by breaking up with them. They hope that their partners might eventually become the person who will give what they want."

4. Men cheat because of selfishness.

"He cares only about himself alone so he can lie without regret if he gets what he wants. His selfishness prevents him from honoring another person above self and ruins his integrity of character and commitment."

5. Men cheat because they have unrealistic expectations.

"Some men who thought that after marriage their life would be great become disillusioned with their marriages when they have to take responsibilities and take care of other people and their needs. They believe that their partners should meet their whims and desires 24/7 and fail to understand that their spouses have lives of their own and may have other priorities (*children, home, finance, work*). When their expectations are not met, they start looking for intimate attention elsewhere because they think that they deserve to be happy."

6. Men cheat because they lack admiration and praise and when they do not feel valued.

"Men like to be praised spontaneously and genuinely. They work hard for their families and would like to receive appreciation and attention; if their emotional needs are not met and they are constantly ignored or criticized, they may feel neglected and emotionally disconnected from their partners and lack intimacy in their marriage. Then, they consider an affair as an opportunity to receive approval, admiration, attention that makes them feel good. This is probably one of the most common reasons why men cheat."

7. Men cheat because the relationship is losing excitement.

"If a relationship gets monotonous, it may feel like a burden. If you feel bored in the relationship, it is just a matter of time before one of you start looking for opportunities to make your life more exciting. Men often have affairs to escape from the routine of everyday life and have a new experience or some adventure. They are looking for thrill, excitement, and novelty."

8. Men cheat because they are confused about love.

"Some men fail to understand the evolution of love in healthy long-term relationships. They do not understand that in a truly committed relationship, the rush of early romance is replaced with less intense feelings of commitment, attachment, and emotional intimacy. Men, who focus on the romantic ideal, miss this short and intense phase and start longing for a passion that was present when their relationship began.

There might be a multitude of reasons why men cheat but in fact, most of them really want to be faithful and committed in their relationships. So the main reason for unfaithfulness is that something is going wrong in the relationship."

I believe her reasons are very insightful as I am not married, however I surely can interpret and break down her reasons in accordance to Mr. Gary Neuman's survey finalizing and expanding all possible reasons why men cheat according to the psychology of men as follows, shall we finally begin with the combined data to make five concrete reasons from both *Life Advancer* and Mr. Gary Neuman's findings, combined with my main two reasons men cheat.

CHAPTER NINE

Five Major Reasons Men Cheat

Just in case you might get lost I will bring back the data once more to get right into the five major reasons. These reasons will speak to women and help many to maintain relationships. For further study, please refer to First Volume- Why Women Cheat? Chapter-Seven; Maintaining a Relationship. Results of the survey; "**200%** of the men who admitted to being unfaithful towards their partners, **48%** gave the reason for cheating being "*emotional dissatisfaction*" because men seek praise & Admiration, **40%** find this praise from their colleagues, **88%** cheated with women less attractive than their partners and **77%** were enablers hence, close friendships with other cheaters and only **68%** felt guilty about cheating."

Reason Number 1- **Enablers at 77%**

As already explained in Chapter-Five, the number one reason why men cheat is due to their foundation. The way a man is raised determines the outcome of his life. I was raised and surrounded by cheaters who had no empathy for women and so subconsciously that became a part of who I was. As **Mr. Gary** puts it in his own words, *" 77% were enablers hence, close friendships with other cheaters."* He goes on to explain in his book that the men only cheated from seeing their friends doing it.

Reason Number 2- **Lust at 88%**

According to the data in **Gary's** words, *'88% cheated with women less attractive than their partners."* This clearly shows us the expression that "men are dogs," a very strong saying that women love to express their pain and anger towards men that hurt them bad. To be honest when I was in my right mind never did I sleep with anyone I found less attractive. It used to puzzle me when I saw my close friends sleeping around with ugly women. I remember how I would lecture them, I never understood it not one bit. Whether a man is in a relationship or not he can defile himself with such creatures that appear as if they are from the pits of Hiroshima. Any man that is under the power/ blindness or even veiled by the spirit of lust is victim to sleeping with just any female even a man as explained in chapters above concerning homosexuality.

The spirit of lust does not seek beauty but pleasure in fulfilling its perverted immoral desires through the vessel it possesses. A spirit/demon however you may put it needs a physical vessel to operate its spiritual desires. Throughout my six years of ministry I noticed that the most common demonic cases and reports evolve around sexual spirits and almost all the world have no clue when and how they are being used even if they think life is peachy for them. My Eyes seen things, it is not easy to make it to heaven. **God** says; *"My People perish for lack of knowledge."*

Reason Number 3- Emotional Dissatisfaction at 48%

Please bear in mind that points 1-4 by *Life Advancer* fall under Emotional Dissatisfaction. Research shows that men are sensitive and need to feel wanted. Some women are just full of past relationship baggage, unhealed memories, too much drama and all that just lands on the men which is too much responsibility for him to be both boyfriend, husband and father with a bonus of counsellor. Men in such relationships victims of abuse and the sad part is that it is always the good ones. I have had my fair share of abuse by broken women who cry a lot, and whine and whine it gets frustrating and turns into a negative relationship and that is just mental trauma. Most men at this stage jump into other affairs to feel alive and forget their problems. I have done it twice, when I was under lust, I was very proud of it but upon being set free, I look back and think what the hell.

Reason Number 4- Praise & Admiration at 40%

Points 5 & 6 by *Life Advancer fall* under Praise & Admiration. Having her points in mind now imagine a male with the famous **Peter Pan Syndrome.** "People who don't want to grow up and assume responsibility," due to external factors such as; over protective parents, high cost of living, lack of capacity of developing normal coping mechanisms, and difficulty in finding partners. Research shows that people born in the late 1980's & 1990's are likely to develop this syndrome. These kind of men are prone to drugs and alcohol as a scapegoat from reality and responsibility who prefer dating younger women as older women burden them with responsibility and marriage. Any time commitment gets serious, they run away. They are troubled with keeping jobs, they lack confidence, and they cannot cope with disappointments and want to be surrounded by people at all times.

In such a relationship its highly likely that the men will cheat on several occasions for not feeling man enough and will definitely need a shoulder to cry over as Gary puts it, "**40%** find this praise from their colleagues." With such a man for a boyfriend or husband women are frustrated and feel like they are taking care of a baby to the point they lose track of appropriate speech and forget that he is the man and not the female. Suh relationships are doomed to end unless the man wakes up from the Peter Pan Syndrome and puts an end to flying to ***Wonder Land.***

Reason Number 5- **Evolution of Women at 68%**

Points 7-8 by Life Advancer fall under Evolution of Woman. According to new research starting from 2009, women have become a major work force dominating in society, which means, Women are becoming more active in work in comparison to men. The year 2019, 54% of managers are women in the USA. The female draft requirement was approved by the US Senate Armed Services Committee, which added a provision to its version of the annual defense policy bill that calls for women to sign up with the Selective Service within 30 days of turning 18 beginning in January 2018. Women in US universities are out performing men in nearly all academic fields.

According to Dating Expert **Marcia Chong,** women have a list and she calls it the ***"80/20 principle"*** which contain all her interests/desires in a man. The list can be any number of important things such as fame, money, car, does he drink, smoke etc. This also explains why women who always nag about a man smoking cigarettes is never settled. While she looks to the future, the man is focused on the now and cannot even understand why she nags so much. Such a bad habit just does not fit in her list therefore, at all costs and quarrel's it must go. When you understand why such a list exists its way easier to get the girl of your dreams. From the list, you learn that women are not really into looks but rather material things. Every woman wants a provider, which goes beyond her as she looks for a suitable partner that can take care of her kids.

As a result to the significant change in female evolution there is a decline in the dating life as more and more men are being out performed the need of men in certain roles as the provider is becoming less and less needed as women now work for themselves and can take care of themselves and their children. The dating list in accordance to men being out performed makes it harder for men to settle with a woman, as some men fear a successful woman in the sense that they feel unneeded or their ego cannot take the heat, which makes separation, ultimately the only solution. Women are not the same anymore; education is doing wonders for them and through them Nations will strive.

According to Gender Historian Dr. **Annine van der Meer,** Sexual freedom and harmony changed around 3000 BC, by an enormous climate change i.e. *"The Ice Age,"* which brought about the Norman time creating a male dominant Society. In short women have been dominated, suppressed, silenced and condemned for too long; not only by ancient societies but by every religion. Today women are free and flourishing in almost all areas of life. To conclude on this point, it is only a woman that can destroy a man of

God and it is only a woman that can understand a man of God hence, the reason why church members in almost all diversities of denominations are the women.

To summarize these points in line with Gossip we need to understand the ***Secret-Circle of Information.*** Through their (Women) discussions and the media, they know that Tom and Jerry are a couple thus women respect each other and will not intentionally cross the line to mingle with Tom. Any women that does so is certainly not right in the head and has shameful morals. These women need deliverance from lust. Men do not have a circle but they do have an **Inner-Circle,** which is not as large as the secret circle thus, our communication is limited in comparison. Men simply have no respect for Jerry which is what every women needs to understand.

Men take pride in mingling with Jerry so when you go off and decide to cheat keep this in mind that to Tom you are just another Jerry that your Tom (man) is failing to treat you right, hence the men in this case will most definitely take advantage of the women's emotions. Once the mingling is over you become nothing. However, there are some rare cases where feelings are caught as a result of a Soul Tie, but still why cheat on your man or women when you know very well what a relationship is in the very first place?

What you do now becomes a habit and a very hard one to break in future. If you cannot understand a relationship at the age of twenty then there is no point in jumping into one. Rather be alone and single until you are married or healed from past relationship baggage. A relationship is not something to mingle with like a commodity of spare parts of a vehicle. Your man or women do not come under warranty and can certainly not be replaced when dissatisfied with. We are all human beings and desire love and attention. Both male and female need to be loved, need to feel loved, wanted and desired. Where there is no love there is no relationship. Remember I spoke of Karma earlier on like a joke but believe me what I speak off is no joke. All that you do now comes back to you in future as the saying goes; "what goes up must come down."

CHAPTER TEN

Three Pillars of a Relationship;

Despite the Seven elements of maintaining a relationship there exists three Pillars that support the foundation of a healthy relationship which for centuries have been introduced into the world with a stigma. Allow this Chapter to speak to you without feeling any religious blockage. By this I mean, Adam and Eve were commanded to be "fruitful and multiply the Erath." We all know too well that sex is best enjoyed in marriage as further commanded by God, however when the topic how to please your partner in bed surfaces, what comes to the mind of many is sincere and religious judgment towards the person teaching the subject.

By this what I mean is as follows; because all we ever hear is that sex is wrong and we should only engage in the act once we celebrate holy matrimony we all tend to have this religious wave that acts as an alarm thereby rendering us subconsciously deaf to the knowledge being offered when it comes to the subject of sex lessons in keeping your partner happy. I guess it makes sense to stay away from such knowledge if you are not thinking about marriage but to those thinking about finally settling down it is crucial to learn how best to satisfy your wife or husband for the following three reasons.

Number One: The Balance in Religion

First, we need to understand that God cares who you marry or even the person you dating. Quoting the Bible is Quoting God Himself. Look at this verse "You shall make no covenant with [the people of the land] and show no favor to them. Furthermore, **you shall not intermarry with them…** for they will turn your sons away from following Me to serve other gods..." **Deut.7:3-4** thus, we clearly understand the will of God when it comes to choice in our partners. We need to choose the right woman and the right man. Choosing the wrong partner is disobedience to God which can only mean one certainty; and that is a lifelong strain of bad luck, what you thought would turn out to be sweet romance would turn into a negative relationship and before you know it, you have drifted so far away from God. Repeatedly in Scripture, we see this theme repeated. Two examples are Samson, who repeatedly sought out unbelieving women, a choice which in the end destroyed him **Judges 14**, and Solomon, the wisest man in the world - until his many wives led him to worship other gods **1kings 11**. If Christ is truly King of our lives, our most intimate selves must be submit to His influence. How then can we unite a Spirit- led soul to one in rebellion against God? This rubs people the wrong way, because no matter how respectful, sweet, or "loving" an unbelieving partner is, he/she is at odds with Christ (rebellion). But if we call ourselves Christians, we're saying we believe the Bible is our final authority. The Bible says that all have sinned and fallen short of the glory of God and that without Christ we are "[unresponsive] in our transgressions", conformed to the world, "living by the cravings of our flesh" and "by nature, children of wrath". **Eph.2:1-3** this is who we are without Jesus.

In the end it doesn't matter how many times we try to give that person second chances, the end result is the same consequence of that rebellion which only leads to a negative relationship hence, the balance in religion is crucial for a healthy relationship. To give a practical example, imagine a **Prophet** and a **Prostitute** in a relationship. The same way the spirit of a man craves for God and Holiness at the same time the body desires things of the flesh such as sin and anything not in relation to God, the prostitute with no conviction of who God is would not want to go to church while the Prophet yearns to worship God. A more practical example would be a man and woman; one being an introvert and one being an extrovert. The two would be what the bible terms an unholy union and from that union once a soul tie is formed, it is a series of stranger things.

If we look into **Genesis Chapter 2,** we can decipher the will of God concerning relationships and unto marriage. The first crucial detail to notice is that God made man outside the Garden of Eden **Genesis 2:15** in Theology it is said; Man was created in the wilderness and that explains why man have this wild nature. The point here is from the wilderness man was brought into the Presence of God which is Eden to fulfill the scripture which God declares we were created to Worship Him the Most High God and any man or women who does not know this is lost. The same verse gives the second criteria of a man, which is to cultivate the land i.e. Work (Money). In the following verses being **18** we now find God saying; "*it is not good for men to be alone*" and that's when Eve comes into the picture. God made Adam, the first man on the earth to fall into a deep sleep and removed a rib from the man and formed the women whom God terms a **"Help for Man."** This is the summary of the Three Pillars of a relationship. First, the man or woman must come out of the world and into God's presence and the second thing needed is work and then both the couple can live happily ever after in fruitfulness in all areas of their lives.

Number Two: Financial Standing

There is a saying, **"man is a social animal."** As stated already, cheating starts in the heart as it is a desire to satisfy what is missing in your lover with another person. The more the desire grows the more your mind opens up to the thought of entertaining another person, that is knowingly or unknowingly, you will begin to ponder and eventually plan how best to let the act happen. Now understanding this principle, cheating is not only about sex, as intimacy with another soul is the final act of cheating.

The **"Attention-Factor,"** Is a universal force not be reckoned with. Look at it from this angle. Women who wear **"make-up"** do it due to insecurities as either they see themselves as not beautiful enough or unattractive enough, this becomes an addiction. They crave the comments such as, "you look beautiful." Such a statement however, is different from, "you are beautiful" thus; the insecurity may just never disappear. This does not however fail to justify the males end, as his intentions are to make the female happy with such beautiful words. Now the problem with makeup women is that any Tom may give them the satisfaction they need and this attention is deadly; as such, a female is easily prone to the deceptive words of men. Ladies! Questioning your beauty is the work of the devil. You are "beautifully and wonderfully made" by the Hands of God the Creator of Heaven and Earth.

Now a result of this insecurity the moment the relationship is on the negative stage and the fighting has already commenced, the thoughts of cheating only run rampart and even unchecked. Partners begin to evaluate the negative reasons and wish they chose someone else instead of the problem at hand. This stage applies to married man who find peace at work from their nagging wives in accordance to the survey. Now let us not forget that women also cheat. It is highly common for women to cheat on their man for not having a strong financial standing in comparison to men. This is why money is one of the three Pillars of a healthy relationship. It has been proven that women can easily be silenced by a cheating partner who thinks he can get away with infidelity. Not because he is good at cheating but the fact that he has a good/strong financial standing or even has both the money and fame. Women are more attracted to such men making them a target to infidelity.

Number Three: The Power of Sex

A man was born to be fruitful and so his desire/job is to have sex. ***"Men need sex"*** as stated by **Dr. Myles Munroe** posted on You Tube March 27, 2017. He also stated that; *"men don't want sex, they need it."* As men, we are always ready for some good action but women on the other hand were not born with that purpose and so they tend to give excuses often such as "I'm tired, not today, we are having too much sex." A man and a woman are different in nature and the question of higher sex drive is debatable however in favor of women. The number one reason couples fight a lot namely rounds up to their sex life. To explore the Power of sex let's look at the anatomical differences which tell us that the female clitoris contains 15000 nerve endings and the head of the penis only has 4000 nerve endings. **Dr. Phil** a renowned psychologist some years back stated that the female's orgasm is recorded at **75%** while men only experience at **25%** hence, the reason women are always too tired for sex is that it really drains them of a lot of energy. Remember sex is energy and science has discovered that the transfer of power in the difference of orgasms can kill a male if the female levels were to run in the brain of a male.

The three Pillars in summary are as follows; Sex is a happy (Money), Spiritual (energy), Tri-Dimensional (religious) activity, a place where you can finally let go of all the physical and emotional baggage. In other words the act of sex is saying take my body, my spirit, my soul, take all of me; all my problems are yours now and together we become one. As much as it can be a good thing, it can also be dangerous. I believe all women are the same at the end of the day and that given the chance all can make the very same mistakes. If the sex game is not right for the women who knows her body then chances are high that even a married woman will look outside of marriage for sexual pleasure despite the man having both the money and right religious standing hence, cheating is looking for what is missing in your partner nothing less and nothing more. Forgiveness plays a major role in these hard acts but the question is why you have not been listening to each other in the first place. Listening is key to developing a healthy relationship, which fall under the vitals of communication. Both science and psychology can agree. At some point amidst all the quarrelling couples, simply turn to deaf ears more like create an invisible barrier whereby they become exhausted with the fighting and willingly choose to ignore each other, which becomes the constant norm being the only thing that makes perfect sense to stop all the mental, emotional and physical abuse in the relationship.

Now understanding the three pillars, what they are and how they work, we need to understand that love is not a concept of following your heart as the media portrays this sophisticated love that confuses people. Love is not a strong feeling that overshadows your will of reasoning but love is the actual will power in choosing whom to love. This concept of love being a romantic movement that both the man and women have no power over is a fallacy that leads many relationships straight into negativity and curses. According to **Jeremiah 17:9** "the heart is deceitful above all things and desperately wicked, who can know it." **Verse 10** goes on to explain that only God knows what exactly is in the hearts of men. Remember the duty of the heart is to pump or circulate blood to the rest of body not feelings so any feelings felt in the heart is a malfunction and emission of lust, which is a wicked feeling and cannot be trusted.

It is important to remember that love is primarily an action word in the Bible, not an emotion. Paul tells us in **1 Corinthians**, "Love is patient, love is kind. It does not envy, it does not boast, it is not proud. It is not rude, it is not self-seeking, it is not easily angered, and it keeps no record of wrongs. Love does not delight in evil but rejoices with the truth. It always protects, always trusts, always hopes, and always perseveres. Love never fails" **Chapter**

13. Our faith shows itself in things we say and do and in the way, we treat other people. Jesus once said, "I am the vine; you are the branches. If a man remains in me and I in him, he will bear much fruit" **John 15:6**. We are told in **Galatians** those fruits include, "love, joy, peace, patience, kindness, goodness, faithfulness, gentleness, and self-control" **Galatians 5:22**. When we see these fruits of the

Spirit in our lives as Christians, when we see love in action, it gives us a certain amount of confidence that our faith is genuine and that the love of Jesus really is dwelling in our hearts and influencing the way we live.

Now knowing this it is very surprising that a lot of women do the opposite concerning the will of God when they leave the Church which is the Presence of God and go to the wilderness i.e. the world in search of husbands only to force them to church of which many do not go. Why would women do this to themselves? The bible is clear; "you cannot force a donkey to drink water." Not to interpret that men are donkeys nor are they dogs. Everyone in this walk of life has their own struggles and cheating under the manipulation of the Demon of Lust is a bigger problem than it appears to be normal. In fact from my personal experience and understanding having a Demon of Lust is a curse that comes with a lot of enjoyable sex, which makes it appear to be a very fun life when in fact there is nothing pleasing about a perverted life, which is unclean in the eyes of the Most Holy God.

CHAPTER ELEVEN

The Curse of Fornication & Adultery

What is fornication? From the world dictionaries fornication means;

Sexual intercourse between two people not married to each other. The word fornication as used in the Bible carries a different meaning than in world dictionaries. As seen in Bible history and its translation, the Old Testament was first, written in Hebrew. The Old Testament uses two Hebrew words for fornication.

"*Zanah*" meaning sexual immorality or idolatry

"*Taznuth*" meaning idolatry.

The New Testament was first written in Greek and the Greek word for fornication used is '*porneia*' meaning sexual immorality. Therefore, the word **fornication** in the Bible is used to mean either **sexual immorality or idolatry.** Sexual immorality covers all illicit or unlawful sex (sex that does not conform to accepted morals). This includes adultery, homosexuality, bestiality, incest, sexual intercourse with false gods, prostitution or harlotry, whoremongering, etc.

Some Bible versions use the word 'sexual immorality' instead of the word 'fornication'. Bible translators did this but the original word is fornication.

Pre-marital sex

The Bible does not speak of 'pre-marital sex' in any place and the usage of the word fornication does not mean 'pre-marital sex'. There is 'pre-marital sex' in the world but in the Bible, in the eyes of God, there is no 'pre-marital sex'.

Why? This is because when two people have sexual intercourse, they become one flesh thus, husband and wife in the eyes of God. Gen 2: 24 "therefore a man shall leave his father and mother and **be joined to his wife and they shall become one flesh. This is marriage according to the bible.** Gen 2: 25 "and they were both naked, the man and his wife and they were not ashamed." The certificates, weddings etc. do not constitute a marriage in Gods eyes but the eyes of men. Such certificate are Contracts of Marriage by the World System of Laws and Regulations by the State Government.

I remember back in college when I was pursuing a certificate in Paralegal Course I met a girl whom I liked a lot in fact I chose to love her so much that we both wanted to marry even though both sides of the family were against it. The more we talked and thought of marriage the idea finally settled in my spirit and I knew then what I needed to do. After a sincere investigation I discovered marriage according to the system of men was a big lie and nothing biblical so I decided to seek God myself knowing the anointing I carry, she later told me of a dream she had in which she was told to marry me and every detail of the dream was prophetic and true. To be honest lust ruined that relationship despite me not having an affair or cheating.

When a man has sex with his wife and both are naked, they are not ashamed. However, when a person is committing adultery or fornication and they are both naked, they are ashamed. Many people's conscience are corrupted thus; they are not ashamed of their sins and are prostitutes in the realms of the spirit. The thing with actual prostitutes is that they do not feel any shame and can open their legs to any man whether he be a child or an adult, ugly or handsome, tall or short even fat or skinny their legs will open. One thing many men do not know about prostitutes is that despite the fact that they open legs, they hate men and some distribute the deadly virus on purpose. Many especially in countries where black magic is common, use charms on men to get their way, in the rarest of cases some who have died, their spirits torment men that have slept with them when living.

It is amazing the number of men that love getting intimate with prostitutes, for these men I can quote, "My People perish for lack of knowledge." As stated earlier on, men cheat because of two main factors, the first being how they were raised and the second being lust. Prostitutes carry very strong **Demons of lust** that trigger men to find no rest until they get intimate with them and form soul ties that disrupt their marriages and even thinking. The moment a men sleeps with a prostitute he has opened a door to the demonic realm where unseen attacks occur. Some of these problems only go by a prayer of deliverance. Some men lose all focus on their marriage and begin to live with the prostitute as his wife giving all attention to a stranger manipulated thinking his in love.

Diseases Born of Fornication:

The spiritual danger of the sexually immoral is rejecting Jesus and perishing in hell as a lost sinner. The physical danger of the sexually immoral is disease, torment, and a shortened life span. There are all kinds of diseases out there ready to infect those who disdain the monogamous sexual relationship in marriage. In fact, there are so many diseases that most people do not even know the extreme danger they place themselves as they fornicate from partner to partner. Yes, everyone has heard of AIDS and this plague is a great killer of the sexually immoral. Besides AIDS, many diseases can kill and torment a person.

HIV & AIDS:

The first disease we will examine is the very well-known plague of AIDS. This disease has gotten lots of publicity in the last 10 years. Unfortunately many people know about AIDS and are blind to all the other diseases besides AIDS. Here is some information on this plague of AIDS. Description: AIDS is caused by strains of a virus, known as HIV (human immunodeficiency virus). HIV attacks certain white blood cells called T4, or CD4, cells. The virus is spread through the exchange of body fluids (semen, blood, and blood products). Sexual fornication is a great way to spread the disease. Other ways to become HIV positive is by tainted blood and blood transfusions. This type of infection has been very dangerous as the blood supplies that are used by hospitals have been contaminated by the AIDS virus. Drug use using dirty needles or a nurse or doctor accidently stabbing themselves with an infected needle or scaple is another way to get AIDS. Symptoms: AIDS can develop in the body for a decade or more without any visible symptoms. The disease weakens the body's immune system allowing other diseases to attack the body. As the immune system breaks down the body can be attacked by cancer, pneumonia, skin disorders, rashes and other problems. A test may be performed to see if the person is infected with the HIV virus. Most people who are HIV positive do not know it. As they fornicate they freely expose others to the disease.

Notes: Since AIDS can remain undetected for ten or more years a HIV positive person can freely spread the disease as he fornicates. AIDS is a fatal disease which will eventually kill the person who has it. Death comes by complications and diseases related to the breakdown of the body's immune system. The person usually does not die directly from AIDS but from the other complications and sicknesses from a destroyed body immune system. This disease is a killer. If you get it, you are dead. I hope you are ready to stand before God as there is no cure for AIDS. Since the virus easily mutates it will be virtually impossible to cure. As soon as a cure is found the virus will simply mutate to another form to bypass the cure. AIDS is a deadly plague which should be avoided at all costs. The sad thing about AIDS is that it is spreading rapidly. As the number of infected people increase the danger of innocent victims contracting this disease also increases. Innocent victims have already been infected by tainted blood or even from going to a dentist that does not properly clean his instruments. AIDS is truly one of the last day's plagues upon the earth.

HERPES:

Description: It is a contagious viral infection affecting the genitals and mouth area of men and women. It is caused by the Herpes Simplex-2 virus (HSV-2). Another form of Herpes is caused by the Simplex-1 virus (HSV-1) and affects a person from the waste up with blisters and cold sores. This disease can be transmitted by contact with an infected person's genitals (HSV-2) or by a person's mouth that has sores and blisters (HSV-1). Symptoms: Painful lesions or sores that keep reappearing. With HSV-2 the sores are below the waist. With HSV-1 the sores are above the waist.

Notes: Herpes is very contagious and currently in North America one person in six have the disease. Since it is a virus based sickness the body's immune system fights this sickness. As a result the body may be weakened and in danger of other forms of infections and diseases. There is no cure for herpes. Once a person gets this disease they must live with it the rest of their lives. I've heard the term used to describe this disease: 'Herpes are forever!' It is not a fatal disease but it certainly is an infectious and uncomfortable disease to live with. It is best avoided.

The next disease we will look at was a big problem back in the sexual revolution of the 60's. However this disease has not gone away and a person can still be infected with this disease as they fornicate.

SYPHILIS:

Description: caused by the spirochete Treponema pallidum. It is contracted by sexual contact as person fornicates with an infected person. Symptoms: A chancre or a skin ulcer, eruption of the skin and mucous membranes, inflammation of the eyes, bones, and central nervous system. This disease can damage the heart and aorta. If not treated, there can be central nervous system damage which could lead to blindness and insanity.

Notes: Syphilis is treated with Penicillin. However there are now resistant strains that cannot be cured. This is dangerous as many types of syphilis can be treated but others are incurable. I guess it is the 'luck of the draw' to see which type you will get if you are fornicating. Maybe you will get the type of syphilis that cannot be cured or maybe you will get the type that responds to drugs. If you are an immoral person then prepare to enjoy your time with terrible diseases like syphilis. The next disease was also quite popular with the sexual revolution of the 60's. However this disease, like syphilis, is still present today.

GONORRHEA:

Description: Gonorrhea is a sexually-transmitted disease (commonly known as "the clap" among the hip) caused by the bacterium Neisseria gonorrhea. Areas of the body that can be infected are the genital areas, the mouth, the throat, and the anus. Sexual contact with any of these areas on an infected person can expose a one to the bacteria.

Symptoms: Vaginal discharge, increased urinary frequency, and urinary discomfort (dysuria), lower abdominal and pelvic pain, fever, sore throat, painful sexual intercourse, generalized symptoms of bacterial infection, and sterility.

Notes: Approximately 50% of women with gonorrhea have no symptoms of the disease. So they freely and unknowingly spread the disease as they fornicate. Gonorrhea is often associated with the presence of other sexually-transmitted diseases. Many times these diseases are a package deal. You get several at a time instead of just one! There are also forms of the disease that cannot be cured. Again it is luck of the draw for the fornicators to see what type of disease you will contract! Ask yourself the question the next time you fornicate: 'Do I feel lucky today?' The next disease is one many people have not heard about at all. But this disease is out there and ready to infect the fornicators.

CHLAMYDIA:

Description: Caused by microorganisms that live as parasites within a cell (Chlamydia trachomatis). These microorganisms have properties in common with both viruses and bacteria. Transmitted by sexual contact with an infected person.

Symptoms: The majority of people with chlamydia are without symptoms until complications appear. In men, the symptoms are similar to gonorrhea. Remember several of these diseases come as a package deal. You just don't get one but you get several diseases at a time! Symptoms for men are: burning with urination, discharge from the end of the penis, tenderness or pain in the testicles and lower abdomen and fever and chills. For women, Infection can lead to pelvic inflammatory disease (PID). This can cause scarring of the fallopian tubes and sterility. Other symptoms are: urinary burning, increased urinary frequency, and a mild urethral discharge. Sounds like a fun disease doesn't it! Doesn't it make a person just want to go out and fornicate and risk contracting these problems? In addition, there are three strains of chlamydia that are responsible for another sexually-transmitted disease, called lymphogranuloma venereum. This disease is a cause of proctitis and colitis (inflammation of the lower intestine).

Notes: Many times people with gonorrhea are also infected with chlamydia and tests for both should be performed. Treatment is with antibiotics. In women, once PID develops, one out of five will become infertile. Here is some other interesting news about this disease: About 70% of individuals infected with chlamydia do not know they have an infection! Until symptoms appear most do not know they have the disease. Remember that fact if you are a lost sinner and are heading off to a night of fornication.

Next we have a disease that not too many people know about. However it is out there in the world of fornication and immorality for all too freely partake.

HUMAN PAPILLOMAVIRUS:

Description: Passed by sexual contact as people fornicate from partner to partner. Symptoms: A family of more than 60 viruses that cause various growths (warts). The warts can be removed but often reoccur. These warts are often associated with cancer of the cervix, vulva, vagina, and penis.

Notes: Not a well-known sexually transmitted disease but certainly one to avoid! Re-occurring warts is not a good thing to have. Especially if those warts are on the genital areas of a person's body and can lead to cancer.

TRICHOMONIASIS:

Description: a sexually transmitted disease caused by the parasitic protozoan Trichomonas vaginalis. Symptoms: In men it can infect the urethra and bladder. For women it can cause urinary tract infection and cause pain in the genital area. There can also be a foamy, irritating discharge.

Notes: This disease can be treated with a drug called metronidazole. Again, the best cure is prevention. In fact, prevention is the best cure for all these sexual diseases. In this life, we have enough problems. There is really no need to go out and look for new ones.

SCABIES:

Description: Scabies is a skin infestation by small parasites called itch mites. They are transmitted by close body contact with another person during a sex act. In this case, simply touching a person with the mites (handshake) could cause an infection. This is one problem where a person can get infected by touch - sexual or not. The mite lays eggs in the skin of the infected person. As the little bugs hatch from their eggs, they are hungry. They feed like crazy on the infected person's tissue causing severe itching and irritation. A new generation of mites is produced about every three weeks.

Symptoms: Intense itching, which begins one month after the initial infestation. Heavy scratching can lead to bacterial infections.

Notes: A lotion containing permethrin or lindane spread on the skin easily cures the condition. At any rate who wants little bugs growing, eating, and hatching eggs on your body?

The next disease we will look at is Hepatitis. There are many strains of this virus but some of them can be passed by sexual contact. This puts the sexual fornicators in danger of contracting this disease.

HEPATITIS:

Description: inflammation of the liver caused by viral infection. There are several strains of the hepatitis virus. Hepatitis B & C can be transmitted by sexual contact. Other ways to get Hepatitis is through infected blood(transfusion, sharing drug needles etc.). Symptoms: Symptoms include fever, loss of appetite, muscle pains, tiredness, and jaundice. Notes: Hepatitis cannot be cured. Over time, it will damage the liver and cause premature death. This is one to avoid at all costs.

More warnings about fornicating and adultery:

Proverbs 6:24-35 24. "To keep thee from the evil woman, from the flattery of the tongue of a strange woman. **25** Lust not after her beauty in thine heart; neither let her take thee with her eyelids." What I have learned concerning women is that a woman is sent either from God or from the Devil and if she is sent from God she is a Blessing but if God forbid she is sent from the workers of Darkness then she is a curse in disguise of a blessing. In a world where we do not really know it all, the best advice is the Word of God and according to Proverbs, such evil women carry lust a demon you simply cannot resist as a man with tender needs flee from that desire. The book of Proverbs further describes these type of women as **Proverbs 7:5**, "that they may keep thee from the strange woman, from the stranger which flattereth with her words."

These are strange women. Women you do not know whom you become intimate with are very dangerous, with very malicious intentions for your life. Sex is not only about power and enjoyment in the wrong hands sex is dangerous as it is draining. Some women through the occult and demonic possession suck the life out of men and some men too are tasked with the same agenda. Some of the women we see in the streets are not even real human beings but Marine spirits that want to marry you and in the end destroy your life. These kind of deadly agents are common in Universities; they pose as normal human beings and move around fornicating from person to person-sucking energy. The most common targets for Marine Spirits are men of God, as they love draining the anointing to send to false prophets. These wicked spirits do everything in their power to keep their victims blinded from the truth concerning their real identity.

Once God opens your eyes from the blindness that veils you in the form of lust which many mistake for love, the person you sleep with becomes detestable in your eyes. You begin to see everything as clear as day. One physical sign of a Marine Spirit in your life is the fact that the person is a *"Strange Woman or Man"* who appear out of nowhere and they make possible by all means, for you to fall into the dangerous trap of fornication. A soul tie, is easily created by these type of spirits. The scariest and hardest to deal with are the *vessel ones* who have no idea that they are possessed in the first place. Then again, it is very hard to tell the difference once the Marine Spirit shows itself to you.

From experience, this battle is not easy. They are the causes of extreme negative relationships, which reach a point you can be in and out of hospital checking for HIV, which is never found. No trust at all between partners, there is a very high price to pay when it comes to free sex and one major sign of Lust be it in the man or woman, is a lot of free sex is at your disposal. Men and women just undress for you like there is no tomorrow. There is never an end to the supply so men need to understand this point, as of today the dating game has changed its no longer cool to sleep around as we used to some years back. Today it is highly certain that many have slept with demons without even realizing. Wet dreams are found in both men and women and this is factual spiritual evidence of a Spiritual wife and even Husband who are already attached to human bodies. The fact that people dream about having sex only shows that the Spirit no longer needs a host to possess in order to sleep with you, it comes directly as it pleases or rather put when it needs its pleasures fulfilled.

If we were to make a survey on the number of people who experience wet dreams the results would be shockingly high and would be something like this; out of 100% we would find that 60% find comfort and great pleasure from their experiences because science has deemed it normal and okay. 20% would be Christians who know what exactly is happening to them and out of that 20/12% would be frightened and give more violent detail of the physical attacks and violent spiritual rapes that take place in the middle of the night leaving them frightened of the long nights as well as emotionally and spiritually broken. A great number would be females. The remaining 20% would agree that it happens occasionally, not too often to even take note of it and would be honest enough to state that they do not understand it at all.

Final Remarks

PREVENTION OF SEXUAL DISEASE:

There are only two ways to prevent an infection from a terrible sexual disease. The first is abstinence from sexual relations. The second is a faithful marriage relationship. There is really no other way. Condoms certainly are not the answer. The lost sinners claim that by just wearing a condom you are protected and can have 'safe sex' with your many partners. This is a lie. People still get pregnant even though a condom is used. The AIDS virus is much smaller than a sperm cell and can easily pass through the many defects in a condom. In addition, it is possible to transmit a sexual disease by close contact and even by kissing.

Gonorrhea for example, does not always manifest symptoms and it can infect the mouth area. A person can be infected by a good kiss to the lips and mouth area. Never-the-less the lost sinner and sexually immoral goes from partner to partner without understanding the dangers of sexual diseases. Many people must have some kind of invulnerability complex or an "it-wont-happen-to-me' type of attitude. Well, I have to let you know, if you play with fire, you will burn. It is as simple as that.

Both men and women cheat because there is a lack in the partner but men cheat due to two main reasons being upbringing and lust. If a woman cheats, it is mainly the males fault for letting it happen. It is easier to catch the man and not as easy to catch the woman, as they are better at cheating due to social and historical reasons that led to stoning and violent deaths hence, women have evolvedover the centuries.

Fornication is not something to be taken lightly and the impact it has on our lives is more sincere than we know. Sexual immoral Spirits exist nothing fiction about them and soul ties leave us broken and lost. To avoid negative relations; we need to listen to the warning signs and make the right choices when selecting partners. Remember not to rush into any relationship, while bearing in mind that the diseases mentioned above most of them are actually demons/spirits that follow fornication, which explains why the majority of them have no physical treatment.

In the bible, Jesus rebuked a fever out of a sickly woman, which openly and clearly tells us that some sicknesses are the works of demons and they operate under the type of demon called spirit of infirmity. Some of these diseases are nothing more than deadly plagues because of sin. If you notice nicely that some churches the men of God a very strong enough to remove these deadly plagues once a person has fully repented from their old ways of sinfulness.

We see the mind of **GOD** in **Deuteronomy 22:22 English Standard Version** "If a man is found lying with the wife of another man, both of them shall die, the man who lay with the woman, and the woman. So you shall purge the evil from Israel." There are grave demons that follow such abominations hence a majority of people with all these terrible and deadly diseases are without a doubt very stubborn wicked people whom the wrath of God is evidently upon them.

One of the worst ways to leave behind this world is by sickness and accidents. Do not let this be you. There is a Godly way of existing this world in peace and received in Heaven. Both these worlds are very real and so is Hell. I have been there once and asked God never to return, there is nothing pleasant in Hell.

Genesis 20:2-3 New Living Translation 2 Abraham introduced his wife, Sarah, by saying, "She is my sister." Therefore, King Abimelech of Gerar sent for Sarah and had her brought to him at his palace. 3 But God came to Abimelek in a dream one night and said to him, "You are as good as dead because of the woman you have taken; she is a married woman." First point to note is that Abraham lied in fear of his life; he knew well enough they would kill him for being the husband of such a beautiful woman, in order to escape death, he lies by stating she is his sister. Second point to note. Even though he lied the wrath of God was on pharaoh for taking a married woman, and to make things worse one that belongs to a man of God, a vessel that God Himself was using mightily. Third point to note is that God declares "you are a dead man." So many people are dead men walking and they have no clue about it. Pharaoh did not die because he repented and pleaded with God arguing in truth that he never knew she was married.

Last, there is no such thing as a soul mate. It is the man's duty to build the woman into the image he desires the same way God worked on the making Adam into His likeness and Image so too do we need to discipline ourselves into forming the woman of our choice into our likeness and image, no one else will do it for you. It is our role as the man to take on this responsibility and not fall weak in the process.

References

David J Ley Ph.D. Published May 19, 2010 viewed on Sunday 11 February (2018)

psychologytoday.com/blog/women-who-stray/201005/ why-are-women-cheating-more

AARP Sex Survey Published May 07, 2010 viewed 12

February (2018)

http://www.foxnews.com/story/2010/05/07/aarp-sex- survey-it-all-downhill-after-45.html?=

Jagran Post Editorial Published on 31 Aug 2012 & Cited on 12 February (2018)

http://post.jagran.com/women-more-forgiving-about-infidelity-than-men-survey-1346399957

https://www.moralrevolution.com/blog/7-signs-of-an-unhealthy-soul-tie

https://www.lifeadvancer.com/why-men-cheat/

http://www.ministeringdeliverance.com/breaking_soul_ties.php

https://tolovehonorandvacuum.com/2014/05/breaking- soul-ties/